Mr Bitcoin

Mr Bitcoin

How I became a millionaire at 21

Mpho Dagada

First published by Jacana Media (Pty) Ltd in 2018

10 Orange Street
Sunnyside
Auckland Park 2092
South Africa
+2711 628 3200
www.jacana.co.za

ISBN 978-1-4314-2672-0

Design by Shawn Paikin and Maggie Davey
Editing by Megan Mance
Proofreading by Linda da Nova
Set in Sabon 11/16pt
Printed and bound by ABC Press, Cape Town
Job no. 003235

See a complete list of Jacana titles at www.jacana.co.za

Contents

Part One

ONE

From birth

Ifirst encountered the world of risk when my mother took a leap of faith. Little did my family realise that this would be the first of many leaps that I would take, broadly, in the realm of business. This is how she told me the story: robbers carrying AK 47 assault rifles were chasing her – and she had to run for both our lives. My mother tossed me into the air, hoping that I would land, alive, on the other side of a three-metre-tall fence. My uncle was on the other side of the fence, with his heart beating fast and his arms wide open, ready to catch me. My life depended on that catch, and I landed right into his hands. This was by far the most terrifying experience I have ever endured, but I was just one year old, too young to understand the horrific events of that day.

My grandfather, Richard Dagada, and my grandmother, Mutshekwa, lived in a small, remote village called Matshavhawe in Venda, Limpopo. This was in the 1980s when the apartheid system was still at its peak. Limpopo is a province well-suited to farming, and that is why many people settled there to work the land. Matshavhawe is right next to the main road that leads to the town of Makhado, then known as Louis Trichardt. The forerunners of apartheid found that the strip of land at the edge of Matshavhawe was ideal for avocado farming, so they ordered all the black people who lived in that village to move further up the mountain, so the whites could occupy the good land and grow avocado pears.

Moving further up the mountain meant that the villagers were far away from the main road where farming was more feasible. And it was a tricky business to come down from the misty mountain and carry on as an active farmer. Life on the mountain turned out to be very difficult. Many villagers had to go without their crops and livestock. My grandfather was intelligent, and as the man of the house, he felt that it was his responsibility to provide for his family. He saw an opportunity which would bring in some money for the family, took the risk and opened a small shop where he sold household essentials. This provided him with the income he needed to survive. He would travel 40 kilometres from Matshavhawe to the town of Louis Trichardt to buy stock for his shop, then come back to the village and offer it for sale. Once the inventory ran out, he would return to Louis Trichardt and restock the shop, at least once a week. This was a routine that made him the busy man he was. It wasn't easy to run the business alone. Between being a businessman and a family man, my grandfather had to find some balance in his life.

He was the mastermind behind the business, but my grandmother managed the shop. They complemented each other perfectly. They were always looking out for one another and always holding the other's best interests at heart. Grandmother Mutshekwa was a hard-working, courteous woman who created a relationship of solid trust with her customers, which attracted more clients to the business. Her strength resonated throughout the warm home she built for her family. My grandmother was an outspoken woman with a sturdy nature. She owned many dogs that she treated well, and they repaid her kindness with the protection they provided for the household. Every villager knew that my grandmother could not be disrespected in any way because if she did not retaliate, the dogs would. My grandfather held her involvement in the business in high regard; he appreciated the work and effort she put into it. Their strong personal and professional relationship was fuelled by the respect they showed one another.

Grandmother Mutshekwa was a hard-working, courteous woman who created a relationship of solid trust with her customers, which attracted more clients to the business.

Within a short time, the business thrived, and the family was accumulating substantial cash. This inspired my grandfather and made him think of new avenues to expand his business. He was a man of action. Every time he put his mind to something, he would go all out to make sure that he fulfilled his desire. I admired this trait in him, an admiration that is with me to this day.

He decided that the next best step would be to set up a franchise in the nearest village, called Hamaelula. He dreamed of running the same business he operated at Matshavhawe in this new village. Hamaelula was about 15 kilometres from Matshavhawe, linked by a gravel road, so it was difficult for him to move between the two villages. But this challenge was no barrier to his success. My grandfather made it work and he charged forward with his goal in mind.

He had a clear vision of how he wanted his business to run in Hamaelula. He knew that just as in Matshavhawe, one of the main ingredients for a successful business is efficient management. As a manager, my grandfather had power, and he knew that it was entirely up to him, to channel that power in such a way that he would build a lasting reputation for himself.

It is a businessperson's responsibility to ensure that the systems that are put in place will make the business run efficiently whether the owner is present or not. This is a belief that my grandfather viewed as of great importance. He needed someone he could trust to manage the shop in his absence. He needed a team that would put in as much effort into his business as he did – even without him there to hold their hands all the time. My grandfather was not always physically present to oversee the day-to-day running of his business. But he had a great team and he knew they would get the job done when he was away. I learned so much from watching my grandfather. He knew how important it is to be aware that the characters within a team demand different managerial styles. You must always consider the people first. If you know the type of people you are dealing with, then managing them becomes easier. Balance is key; like Grandfather, don't be too authoritative – and at the same time don't be too soft. It helps to relate to employees as people first, before you relate to them as staff you hired to work for you. This enables trust and respect between employer and employee.

People who are envious of your success will try to undermine it in whatever way is available to them, often through trying to damage your reputation.

The young Richard Dagada decided to look for a candidate who would best suit the shop manager position. But he found more than that – Grandfather found a wife! And together they made the shop everything he had hoped and fought for it to be. It was no secret that Grandfather was polygamous. His ability to take on more than one responsibility was not only demonstrated in business, but it manifested itself in his love life as well. Although these responsibilities were heavy at times, my grandfather handled all of them with great care. His spirit carried him through all his successes.

With his second shop it became evident that more stock was needed, but the individual trips to Louis Trichardt were both costly and time-consuming. So he decided to buy a truck, which would allow him to bring back much more stock at a time. In those days, owning a truck was a big deal in the black community because it was a sign of prosperity. It was a sign that you were becoming successful; that you were someone important.

The villagers saw that he was becoming wealthier, and as it is with human beings, some were not happy about his achievements, because they could not understand how he had accumulated so much wealth in such a short period. Many would start rumours intended to derail people's admiration of him. These falsehoods were born out of a community's jealousy. This is a common occurrence in the business world. People who are envious of your success will try to undermine it in whatever way is available to them, often through trying to damage your reputation.

As a young, ambitious man, my grandfather desired more shops, more money, and more wives. He saw no limit to success and believed that no goal is reached without it presenting an opportunity to take it another step further. There was always room for more growth. He moved on to a third village, where he opened another shop. As with the first two villages, he got married to a third wife, who handled the day-to-day management of the business. At the end of it all, he had married seven wives, and owned seven shops. He fathered more than fifty children, who produced hundreds of grandchildren and great grandchildren.

Envy continued to rise among some villagers. They could not accept that a man who once had nothing and had been an ordinary villager was now a wealthy businessman, who owned seven shops. Villagers knew that my grandfather never stayed in one village for long. He would spend one day of the week in one village, with one wife, and the next day in another with another wife. My grandmother's day was Thursday.

On Thursdays, she kept a close eye on the household she ruled. Everyone had to be on their best behaviour and the business books had to be in order. She steered us in all directions, maintaining that the children had to have reports ready on what they had achieved that week – be it schoolwork or chores. Although some would say that we were too young to be burdened with such adult-like activities, her system built us as individuals. She taught us responsibility and efficiency. She taught me how to deal with the numbers in the business.

My grandfather would arrive in the afternoon, and the first thing he would do was go to the shop, check the books, check what was running low, and go to Louis Trichardt to buy stock. This efficient routine guided my family to prosperity; a routine that I too have adopted in my life and in the way I conduct business.

My family was big and close. Often we would sit together and bond. Every night, without fail, there would be some twenty people in our Matshavhawe house – servants, family and friends – all gathered together for supper. My grandmother had big pots to prepare the huge meals she would cook for everyone. One night they were gathered in the lounge, laughing and sharing stories about the events of the day. And just like every other night, enjoying the feast that my grandmother had prepared. Within a matter of minutes, the gathering was brought to a tragic halt. They went from laughing and enjoying each other's company, to living through the worst time of their lives.

My grandfather's weekly schedule was common knowledge, and he always arrived late on Thursday evening after collecting supplies in Louis Trichardt. He would come in through the main gate and the security guards would lock up after him. On this day, we heard the security guards shouting outside, 'We have thieves, we have thieves!' Everyone was in distress – anticipating the terror that would follow the security guard's exclamation.

It took a second for everyone to realise that intruders had

broken into my grandmother's home. They broke through the front gate and fired the first shot. There were twenty-one people in the house at the time: my grandfather's employees, his children and grandchildren, including myself. The only thing that everyone knew for sure was that they were in serious danger.

These robbers had clearly done their research. Or perhaps they'd been tipped off by one of the many people who entered the house daily – they knew exactly where my grandfather hid all his money. They knew that he did not use a bank to store it because apartheid-era officials were suspicious of prosperous black businessmen. Another reason for keeping all the money at that particular house was that it was the closest to Louis Trichardt and therefore his main base for purchasing supplies.

While the others were making their way out of the house, there I was – a helpless one-year-old who needed protection. My mother picked me up, and ran for both our lives, as everyone squeezed and pushed through the back door. Everyone ran for the fence because the main gate on the other side of the house was the one that the robbers had used to come in. As people were jumping, one after the other, my mother stood there holding me – feeling helpless and frightened for us both.

My mother was distraught. She was forced to make the toughest decision a mother could make. She couldn't climb over the fence while carrying me and she couldn't wait for us to die there. So she decided to throw me over the fence first, then follow. My uncle was on the other side, ready to catch me. As a practising nurse, my mother knew what the implications would be if my uncle didn't catch me. She knew that I could suffer severe injuries and perhaps become paralysed for the rest of my life. She stood by the fence for a little while, not knowing how to do what she had to do. At that moment, she heard more gunshots – confirmation that she had no choice but to throw me over. She hurled me as high as possible, with all her might, and hoped I would make it. Her heart stopped for a while as she watched her one-year-old son tumbling through the air. She knew that a three-metre fall onto hard ground would hurt me badly. My uncle knew it too, but he kept the faith – and managed to catch me.

He could have thrown in the towel and called it a day – but he didn't. He built himself up and started again. He started bigger and he started better, with caution and with the same care as before.

There was no time to enjoy the relief. My mother had to climb over the fence and join the rest of the family. In the process she broke her arm. As soon as she landed, she and my uncle ran to the neighbouring house. As my mother has often told her now grown-up son, no night in her life could ever be as terrifying as that one. We were okay. My mother could not stop thanking God that we were alive and that we could all stand together and share our gratitude. Even in the height of that gratitude, something else crippled her and this was the fear that something bad could have happened to my father. She did not know where he was, and she sat there hoping he wasn't in harm's way. Understandably in all the chaos, she had forgotten to check on him. The only police station close to the village was 40 kilometres away, in Louis Trichardt, and everyone knew it would not be of much help to call the police at that time. She sobbed in relief as my father emerged from the bushes, after the robbers made away with all the money they had found in the safe. All the money that my grandfather worked hard for and all the money that he had saved to secure the future of his grandchildren and family – all gone!

It's experiences like these that test a person's character, and these very experiences that also strengthen it. My grandfather had lost a great deal of money and he could have given up. He could have thrown in the towel and called it a day – but he didn't. He built himself up and started again. He started bigger and he started better, with caution and with the same care as before. He has taught me a lot about perseverance. And also about the importance of being so persistent with your dreams that only positive results will come out of that effort.

This experience shaped my mother's beliefs about business; she felt that danger and business are synonymous. She felt that being part of the world that my grandfather created was dangerous – and maybe it was not even worth the trouble. However, when my mother related this story and her feelings to me, I interpreted the danger as risk. And most businesses are built on risk. Risk often allows room to make money, create innovative products and grow a successful business. Perhaps being thrown over that fence triggered something in me, the ability or willingness to take unconventional risks – and the courage to pursue a learning path in creating a successful business.

In this chapter you read about the story of my grandfather's success in business. His career inspired me and gave me my first lessons in management. Handicapped by apartheid injustice, he found a way to get past this obstacle and provide for his family by opening a small store. My grandfather learned useful lessons in management, and knew there's more to business than expensive suits, a voice of authority and the art of instilling fear in employees. He put his skills to good use as he expanded his chain of rural shops. He kept them well-stocked, and set up a family-based operating system, in which his wives were trustworthy managers. He and my grandmother acted as a team to build the business. My grandfather suffered a severe blow when a gang of robbers left him without capital, but he refused to give up, and started rebuilding his wealth from scratch.

CHAPTER ONE: KEY LESSONS

1. Use every opportunity afforded to you to learn and grow. Follow my grandfather's example in using what he learned about management to expand his business – you need to trust the people you put in charge.

2. As my mother discovered, business means danger, but risks are worth taking if they can lead to success.

3. Don't forget the hands that held you during tough times. Either at a moment of physical danger, such as my flight over the fence, or during a financial setback such as the robbery at my grandfather's house.

4. Never let the fear of missing the goal keep you from taking the shot. My grandfather, Richard Dagada, could have eked out a poor living on the mountain, but he wasn't afraid to take a risk by starting a small store to survive under apartheid.

5. After a fall, start bigger and better, as my grandfather did after losing everything in the robbery. The hard lessons in life are the most valuable ones.

TWO

A curious mind:
A successful life!

At the age of eleven, I was already listening carefully to the wisdom imparted by my grandfather and grandmother. I used to dream about the business I would run and was determined to start as soon as I could. Admiration for my grandparents led me to a declaration to myself that one day, I too would make a lot of money. I wanted financial freedom, for I saw the power and influence possessed by a successful person. My grandfather had all of this. Many people in the village loved him, loved speaking to him, respected him, and appreciated his wise words.

There I was, with the privilege of free access to a man of great influence. But I didn't spend as much time with him as I would have liked. He was busy, and he had to share himself among his children, seven wives – and many grandchildren. I would sometimes have to book an appointment just to spend an hour with him. But these were hours I'd cherish, hours that taught me a lot. I'd soak up all the knowledge that he poured upon me every time we got to interact, and I would use it every time I needed inspiration.

My grandfather introduced the word 'investor' to me. He believed in growth and also believed that investment was an important way to increase wealth. My grandfather proved this by showing me the contentment one feels when giving back to the community. Although careful about how he spent his money, my grandfather was not stingy, and he would not let a neighbour starve. My grandmother was the same – every child that my grandfather had with another woman, she would take in and raise as her own.

Richard Dagada had always been a hard worker. As a result, he was not keen on seeing his children idling, so he would always create work for them. He owned a farm in Matshavhawe where he planted avocado trees. This farm was big, and it needed someone to look after it. Who better than his children? As my father would tell me, the tasks that my grandfather made them do on the farm were gruelling. They would sometimes have to spend an entire day on the farm, under the hot sun, working without a break.

As much as my grandfather valued manual labour, he also believed education was important. In the 1980s, he would travel to buy stock for his shops from Indians in Louis Trichardt, and these men influenced his way of thinking. Among them was the owner of Surat Cash and Carry. Mr Surat's friendship with my grandfather grew because of the business he brought to him. They also exchanged knowledge about life. My grandfather would tell Surat about the work his children did on his farm, and he would emphasise that he wanted to teach his children to work hard for themselves. Surat advised him that if he wanted success for his children, he would have to educate them. He made my grandfather conscious of the fact that maintaining 50 children came at a high price, and education added to this challenge. So the perceptive Richard Dagada started thinking of education as an investment.

In those days, education was not a priority for the black community. The men often worked in the mines while the women looked after children and their homes. Few black people made it to university, because of a mindset spread throughout the black community by white people. They convinced blacks that they were nothing more than manual labourers who were put on earth to aid the prosperity of white people. But my grandfather did not fall for this; he made sure all his 50 children reached further education, and all of them graduated. Today, some are doctors, lawyers and accountants.

I used to visit my grandmother during school holidays, and she would make me work in her shop. Just like her husband, she hated an unproductive person. She always made sure that she substituted the temptation to idle around the house with a more substantial activity such as helping out with the business. I was only eight years old when I started handling money in her shop. My grandmother introduced me to an attitude that my entire career would depend on: the respect for money.

At such a young age, she trusted me with her money. This was quite a big responsibility. My cousins and I would all gather at my grandmother's home during the December holidays. These were longer school breaks, and we were excited to be in one space all together. Each morning, we would wake up, clean up, and head to the shop. My other cousins would hide away a few cents as the customers kept flooding in to buy. They would make me promise not to tell. At the age of eight I was too young and innocent to fully realise that what they were doing was wrong. Keeping my promise seemed more important. But as I grew, I realised that they were wrong.

That's the beauty of being business-minded. I have always been able to channel my energy into identifying how I can learn from an experience, even a negative one.

By the time I was enrolled at Louis Trichardt High School, I had read about passive income. I used to ask myself, how can anyone make money without having to work long hours? I had learned that more than half of the world's population work to earn a minimum wage. And it seems that all those millions are happy with twelve pay cheques a year, working nine-to-five, just to stay alive. I wanted more and realised that lack of money would be a barrier to the things I aimed to achieve in life. Some families visit first-world countries for vacations, while others can't even afford to buy new clothes for their children. What is so different about these people? Were some saving more money than they were spending, while others were spending more than they saved? These money dynamics interested me. The curious schoolboy that I was wanted to know more.

I learned the power of the mind and the impact of positive thinking, and I knew I had to stay positive so that positivity could manifest itself in my success. There is great power in what we say to ourselves about ourselves.

We had a teacher who taught us Economics, but he couldn't conceal his racism. As we got to know him, we realised that he wasn't shy about his racism, for he wasn't an employee of the school. He was just a pensioner helping a school in need of an Economics teacher. Possibly in reaction to his racist tendencies I was actually able to glean a lot of knowledge from his statements.

This teacher and I would argue and engage, despite his prejudices, and one day we argued regarding the best investment returns you can get in South Africa. At the time it was around 1% per month from an investment firm if you'd made a sizeable deposit. But he confidently revealed this to us: 'I know of a place where you can get 10% in returns per month – but you black people will never find out.'

This statement weighed heavily on many of the pupils. They felt disrespected by how the exclusion that black people still live through was emphasised – even in this day and age. The whole class swore at the teacher, who swore right back at them. But I remained curious about this place where people got high returns on their investment. That's the beauty of being business-minded. I have always been able to channel my energy into identifying how I can learn from an experience, even a negative one.

He told me that he and a group of Afrikaners had formed a savings club. They invested their money, owned a Spar supermarket and other highly profitable assets – and they would share the profits among themselves. The main criterion for joining this high interest club was being Afrikaans. I found it offensive that in order to join this club you had to possess a trait that was essentially out of your control – race! Apart from making me angry and upset that my parents couldn't join the club, I became interested in similar investments with high returns.

Since my school days, I have read many books about the art of making money, and I discovered that some of the topics are easy to understand from a theoretical point of view, but putting them into practice can be difficult. Every successful businessperson will acknowledge that the road to a successful business is full of hardships and challenges. Success is not for the faint-hearted. As I grew into a young adult, I formed my own opinions. I questioned the system of education. I did not try to undermine traditional education, but I was conscious of the fact that knowledge is not limited to schools. What I appreciate about traditional education is that it introduced me to different possibilities I could explore as I built my career. I focused on school, but during my spare time I was reading about business. I was looking at businesspeople, studying their profiles, and learning about money. I was persistent with my dreams. I held onto every piece of knowledge about the business world that I could wrap my head around – and used it. Even if it came from a racist like my economics teacher.

Branching out and exploring other career paths helps develop a person's understanding of the economy, the world and the workplace. This is a mentality that is vital if you want to be successful.

I always asked myself why some people became rich while others remained poor. It was not long before I discovered that it was all in the mind. Soon, I learned the power of the mind and the impact of positive thinking, and I knew I had to stay positive so that positivity could manifest itself in my success. There is great power in what we say to ourselves about ourselves. On one hand, you may find that poor people have accepted the state of their finances and declare to themselves how poor they are. They fail to realise that their words are the seeds they plant, and that whatever they say manifests in their lives. Rich people declare the opposite. They speak about their wealth, and as a result they attract more money into their lives. It's this kind of knowledge, that you won't find in the traditional education system, that can make all the difference. So I have always pushed myself beyond the school and university curricula. The big question that lingered in my head was: 'What will I invest in?' The driving force behind such an inquisitive mind was my desire to succeed.

Some of the pivotal lessons I carry with me are derived from a book called *Rich Dad, Poor Dad* by Robert Kiyosaki. This book showed me how to move from a place where you are an employee to one where you are accumulating wealth and assets. I would listen to radio shows centred on financial management. I analysed how to make sound investments and how to read stock exchanges. In mainstream education, we are rarely taught how to make money from the career paths we choose. Often, we find ourselves stuck between a degree and a hard place. Branching out and exploring other career paths helps develop a person's understanding of the economy, the world and the workplace. This is a mentality that is vital if you want to be successful. Always push yourself beyond your comfort zone. Sometimes the most important trait for innovative entrepreneurs has got to be the art of asking questions – the right questions that lead to the right answers. The habit of asking questions builds an entrepreneur's thought processes and challenges them, and as a result makes him or her better at what they do. This is by far the most effective method of learning. Curiosity can lead us to the lives we are waiting for, in places that we never thought we would reach.

An entrepreneur needs to be aware that a lot of advantages and disadvantages come with being wealthy. The advantages are all embedded in the influence that you are able to wield once you are wealthy. I learned this by studying my grandfather and parents. Wealth allows you to purchase the things you have always wanted without having a limited budget. Wealth also earns you a seat at the biggest tables in the world. You get to meet people who are just as successful and will help you elevate further. Financial freedom becomes a norm. A wealthy person also has a greater responsibility to society, though, to help uphold the spirit of ubuntu. This I learned from both my grandparents, and how they behaved in their community. Today, I know that the greatest joy you will feel is helping someone who can never pay you back.

It is of utmost importance for young people to be aware of what is happening around them. Many youngsters of today live in ignorance, and this causes many of the world's problems. I agree with the saying that 'ignorance is the most serious disease of mankind and all its ills. Healing is achieved through knowledge.' We are surrounded by good advice and great examples to follow and successful people to learn from, but it's up to each individual to see the learning opportunity and to take it. I have met business people who started off with nothing. I realised that no matter how bad their circumstances were, they were committed to learning the important lessons that helped them become successful individuals. The worst thing people can do is make excuses for their standing in life.

In this chapter I stress the influence my grandparents had on me as a growing boy. Many times we get so busy and caught up in the lives we're leading that we forget to reflect and recall all the moments that have helped shape us into who we are. Invaluable – that's the word I use every time I think of the roles played in my life by my grandparents.

I explain how my positive financial attitudes were shaped by lessons in school, even from someone whose attitude I could not respect. I also stress the reading and research I did on my own account. Keeping an interested, active and curious mind, and being well informed is essential. Had I not been that child who never stopped asking questions, I would not have learned the lessons that my business icons taught me. You can build every answer you get from someone onto another person's answer. This forms a concrete foundation that will support you as you grow. My curiosity and interest in business grew because of my upbringing. I have always known that my exposure to the business world at such a young age was preparing me for my destiny.

CHAPTER TWO: KEY LESSONS

1. Always be open to learning outside the classroom. And read as much as you can outside the curriculum because you will discover new truths, new opportunities.

2. Ask the important questions about your passions until you get the right answers. I asked endless questions in my sessions with my grandparents, talking about business and finance. And one question always led to another as my knowledge grew.

3. Don't serve money, make your money serve you. This is a question of attitude. My grandfather didn't see working hard to earn money as a burden to be endured. Not at all! He saw money as a tool he could use to build a fortune. The right attitude will help a man become rich. And the wrong attitude toward money can trap you in poverty.

4. Always consider the people first. This was the way my grandfather managed his staff. He did not impose his will on them, but rather recruited them as willing followers. And when he was rich at last, he acted charitably and helped people who were struggling. This was one of his greatest pleasures and satisfactions

5. I grew up learning how my grandparents lived their lives in moderation. And now, as an adult and a businessman, I try to counterbalance my passion for business with my religious faith and a concern for the wider community and its needs.

THREE

Lessons from
my parents

Inspired by my father's business, I had the ambition of becoming a schoolboy micro lender. I started off by taking some of my allowance and lending it to peers in need. I would only lend out small amounts because that was all I could afford at the time. My first customer was my older brother's friend who had heard of my new business and urgently needed cash. He promised to return the money with an interest of 20% at the end of the month. We shook hands and sealed the deal. At the end of the month, I went to my brother's friend and asked for my money. He stood tall and strong over the naive teenager that I then was, and said: 'I don't have the money!'

I realised from his tone that there was no way around this statement. I was never going to get my money back from him. Not only because he knew my brother and would call it a favour, but because I was smaller than him and he didn't feel he had to respect me enough to honour our agreement. I stood there and realised I'd made a blunder. I had assumed that I could trust people in conducting business and hope for the best. I had no valuable item to hold against him. I did not have anything of his that would compel him to pay me back. And most importantly, there was no written agreement. My business soon collapsed after that incident, and I have never forgotten the lesson I learned. It showed me the importance of careful research into a business opportunity and how foolish it is to rush in without careful consideration.

I have never forgotten the lesson I learned. It showed me the importance of careful research into a business opportunity and how foolish it is to rush in without careful consideration.

My father was a respected businessman within the community, and he also held a top level executive position for an international investment, savings and insurance group, Old Mutual. As he continued to work for Old Mutual, I often wondered when he would give up his nine-to-five job and focus on running a successful business, as a micro lender, on a full-time basis. My father had often faced difficult questions and requests from his friends, family and associates. They would ask him to assist them with loans or funding for their small businesses. These came as challenging questions to my father, for he already knew their credit was in poor standing because of how little they earned, or the financial decisions they had made. Once a person sees success, others want to get in on the vision, and they want favours. This is a side effect of success – you need to be cautious of the people who want to get by on *your* wealth and want to uplift themselves through you.

People would go to him asking for cash loans. My dad saw this as an opportunity to make money. If they demanded a service, and my dad was in a position to help them – while also earning money – he was going to take that opportunity. So he started as a micro lender. But from the outset my mother was against this type of business. She saw it as a form of usury. My mom was also aware of the dangers of being a 'loan shark'. She only saw this business panning out the same way it had done when intruders came to my grandfather's house.

In a rural society, not many people have bank accounts, and when they need credit, the only available financial service provider is the local mashonisa. He functions as part of the society into which he has been born, and he doesn't lend money to strangers. He knows all his customers, as members of his community. My father's position was that if a teacher had little or no money to put his child through university, a loan could help them. That was Dad's attempt to convince my mother that his business was not only for the sake of the family, because it also helped the community indirectly. He was no shark.

My mother still begged to differ. She maintained that if a parent can't afford to put a child through university, that child should stay at home or go to work. Just like my grandmother, my mother was a strong woman who didn't believe that women should sit at home and wait for a man to provide for them – or determine the direction her future took. She too would go out and seek her own form of business. She took to selling Tupperware in addition to being a nurse. So from an early age, I took strides in learning the most valuable lessons in business and how a business can operate to yield profit – and also failure.

My mother followed a different business strategy altogether. She operated a business selling Tupperware – a home product line that includes plastic containers used to store goods and food. My mother targeted women in her community at different places where they all gathered – church, stokvels and other clubs. She would fill her car with Tupperware products so she could put together displays for her potential clients. The ladies would place their orders, and they would be informed on how much they owed. She would get part-payments from some of the ladies, and the others would promise to pay at a later date. This is a common occurrence when entering into an agreement with someone close to you, be it a family member or a friend – there is a lack of urgency when money must be repaid. People take advantage of the relationship and neglect to respect the business side of things. Fortunately, my mother kept a little black book of all the ladies who owed her money.

I observed the differences between how my father and mother conducted their respective businesses. At the end of each month, people came to my father to collect their valuable possessions which they had used as their safety deposit. As for my mom, she sent out bulk SMSes which followed up on the money the ladies owed her for Tupperware products. Unfortunately this often led to her being avoided by many people.

I engaged with my father on these two vastly different business models. I realised that he conducted business logically, while my mother operated morally. And although some aspects of each method seemed to work in certain situations, my father's way seemed to get the job done more efficiently. His angle was: 'My clients have no choice but to return the money that I have loaned them, because I have something important of theirs that they cannot do without.' This assured him that he would not lose any money to disloyal customers.

My mother believed: 'If a customer wants something, you should give them what they want – they will pay.' She trusted that people had pride that they would therefore want to pay off their debts before it reflected badly on their reputations. However, results showed clearly that this model did not yield any profits. My father's business model surprised me because he could charge an interest rate of his choice, whether it was 10%, 15% or even 20% monthly and people still queued up to ask for loans. This was because his clients came to him as a knowledgeable source. They had acted irresponsibly with their finances, so they had to take what they got. It was that simple. I continued to quiz my dad on his business model. It was fascinating to me that people were willing to pay back more than they had asked for in order to meet immediate needs.

Unfortunately for my father, as people got smarter he started to lose control of his business. They knew the stuff they gave to him could easily be replaced. If he had their IDs and bank cards, they would apply for a new ID and bank card to stop my father collecting the money.

He was hesitant to enter the business world on a full-time basis, but finally answered my teenage questions, and took over a petrol station in Tshikombani, a village in Venda, in the years 2002–2005. I took an interest in the filling station and learned even more about this new business. From the get-go we realised that the petrol business is stagnant, especially in a remote area like Tshikombani. For petrol stations, the primary mode of growth is expansion, and the station could not expand, as yet. In addition, the government sets the petrol price, so you can't make up your own pricing structure. This set a limit to the amount of profit that my father could make from this business.

From an early age, I realised that keeping a positive credit record is important, because banks work within a trust system. In a system that runs everything to do with finance, trust is an important element.

As I became more involved in the petrol station, pivotal questions formed between my dad and me. We started to question why we had to pay franchising fees to a corporate giant in the petrol industry, when all they did for us was supply the petrol. When the company approached him to upgrade the garage at his own cost, he declined to do so, and sourced an independent supplier. My father formed relationships with cheaper petrol suppliers and made 50c per litre. As we got even cheaper suppliers, this resulted in a profit of 60c per litre. The business was still slow but we had identified a tipping point. This was the evening before a petrol price hike, and there was an opportunity to make money. If the government was going to increase the petrol price by 30c per litre, we would buy 140 000 litres at the former price, sell it over the next couple of days at the new price and make a profit of R42 000. In addition, the holidays also presented us with increased profits. As the petrol price went up, so did our margin.

Working alongside my father at the petrol station was exciting because it presented me with lessons I apply in my own businesses today. Realising and seizing opportunities is very important, for each opportunity carries risk. My time at the petrol station inspired me to start my own business. I spent the days after that trying to figure out what line of business I would go into. By this time, I was conditioned to believe that it is entirely possible to run a successful business. It can be done, yet not every entrepreneur has the privilege of growing up in a family like mine. So often they feel that business is difficult and its goals are difficult to achieve. Entrepreneurship is a skill that can be cultivated by an individual through study, practice and seeking mentorship in one's particular industry. Running a business is difficult, but the hardest step you can ever take is getting started. Once you have conquered that step, moving forward becomes much easier with time.

My father's involvement in the financial sector brought core lessons in life and business into our home. From an early age, I realised that keeping a positive credit record is important, because banks work within a trust system. In a system that runs everything to do with finance, trust is an important element. A customer begins a trusting relationship with a bank by building a positive credit record – which is something most people in Mzansi don't have. So my dad's business was fulfilling a need within the financial market for people with poor credit records who could not go to the bank for a loan.

Chapter Three tells the story of my first stumbling attempts to become a schoolboy in business. I had been inspired by how my father and mother operated, with very different approaches. He was practical; she was moral. And in the end, when I assessed which business policy was more successful, my father's hard-headed micro-lending enterprise won out over my mother's soft-hearted reliance on trust. My father ran a service station, and I chronicle some of the ups and downs in that business, which fascinated me during my teens.

CHAPTER THREE: KEY LESSONS

1. I learned a hard lesson as a would-be schoolboy micro lender. But I never made that particular mistake again. Failure provides an excellent education.

2. Trustworthy customers are rare in business. My mother's Tupperware clients were slow to pay, because they were all part of a small rural community and because they knew her they felt no pressure to honour their debt. She found that too great a reliance on ubuntu can eat into profits.

3. My father was a micro lender who insisted on holding something of value as collateral for his loans. This ensured that he made a profit, until some of his clients found a way to do without the items he was holding to secure the loans. Despite the fact that they were blotting their credit records. A good credit record is an asset.

4. Operating a franchise can be a good business, provided the franchisee is prepared to accommodate the expectations from the franchisor. My father was expected to upgrade a rural filling station at his own expense, as well as pay a hefty petrol price. So he made a new plan.

5. Stay alert for opportunities, as my father did by finding a cheaper petrol supplier and strategic buying in advance of a government price hike.

FOUR

My first business

Coming from Venda, I saw Johannesburg as the place where I would fulfil all my dreams. When people spoke about the opportunities that Johannesburg afforded I would always listen attentively. Venda was not like Johannesburg, and I saw this the first day I arrived in the Big City. I remember when I arrived, one of the first things I wanted to buy was a mango. In Venda mangos are plentiful because many farming families have big trees bearing beautiful, delicious fruit. But in Joburg, I was told that a mango costs R10. It was a shocking revelation that in order to survive in Joburg, you had to have money for everything. This place is expensive, I thought, so I'd better start my businesses and gain financial freedom.

As a naive 19-year-old, I was certain that my future included a lavish lifestyle. I was ready to tick all the boxes: excel in my studies, get a job and earn good money that would make me a wealthy man. In my mind, I was a step closer to achieving my dreams. I just needed to gear up and work hard. As we grow, we are taught to dream big. Even if the lesson does not come from home, everything we see on television is an indirect indoctrination into that culture which spends large sums of money on amazing things – and often on unnecessary things.

I remembered the time when my dad had started the micro lending business – he had identified a need in the community and cashed in on it. This was my light bulb moment, and this would be the birth of my new business.

I was in the big city, away from my parents and ready to pursue a future in building wealth. Within a matter of weeks at varsity, however, it became apparent that the money I had didn't go that far in Joburg and I needed to start learning to budget. Because I now had to buy my own groceries and petrol, this meant that I couldn't save as much as I did when I lived with my parents. The comforts that I knew from home were all just a memory. At that moment, I knew I had to grow up and find my own way of making money. In Joburg I had to get used to being a student and doing everything for myself. I moved into a residential complex, Milpark Mews in Auckland Park. Everything was going smoothly until two weeks in, when I had to do my laundry. I took my washing downstairs to the communal laundromat. I was told the going rate was R120 to do my laundry, which was a lot of money at that time. Yet another reminder of how expensive Johannesburg is. There was no other way – I had to take my laundry upstairs and hand wash it. There was no way I could afford this price as a student. And laundry was a challenge because not only did it take longer to wash my clothes by hand – the clothes also took twice as long to dry.

I remembered the time when my dad had started the micro lending business – he had identified a need in the community and cashed in on it. This was my light bulb moment, and this would be the birth of my new business. I decided that I would go around the complex and ask other students how they were doing their laundry. I knew that, just like me, most of them could not afford the basement laundromat. I gathered the information that almost everyone else opted for hand washing. This was an opportunity for me to help these students and in turn, make some money for myself.

I took the money that I had saved and I bought a washing machine. This made me one of the few students who owned a washing machine in the building. I let people use my washing machine for a small fee, thinking I would get some extra money. But soon one washing machine wasn't enough to cope with the demand. So I decided to hire a helper – her name was Beauty. Beauty and I did more than just the students' laundry – we would also take on the task of cleaning their rooms. Soon enough, my neighbours asked Beauty to do their washing by hand because they didn't have a washing machine. This gave rise to the business that I was able to start from that demand. Laundry and cleaning became a valuable source of income.

I was still in my first year and knew very little about the formalities of a business and the industry itself. I was not aware that you have to register a business and also let the landlord of the building know that you are running it on his premises. At the University of Johannesburg, we were given printing credits for printing out study notes and other course material. I used all of the money they gave me to print out little pamphlets advertising the service. I focused on my business and used my middle name, Richard, on the pamphlets:

'Richard's Laundry & Cleaning Service

Contact us to collect your dirty laundry and deliver it clean!'

This was exciting for me. I had my first employee, Beauty, who would do laundry and cleaning, while I managed the business operations and marketing. As Beauty and I prepared to hand out pamphlets, I realised that I had forgotten to write a contact number, and this resulted in me having a minor existential crisis – about being known as 'the guy who does laundry in Auckland Park'. Like most first year students, I worried about my reputation. I wanted to fit in and not draw too much attention to myself as the guy who did laundry.

Although direct marketing was illegal in my building as per the body corporate rules, I didn't know that, and slid pamphlets under the door of each apartment. I later discovered that had the strict landlord found out, he would have evicted me or given me a hefty fine. Milpark Mews is an upmarket building in the bustling suburb of Auckland Park, and the building has six floors with about 20 apartments on each floor. I had to come to terms with the fact that worrying about what people had to say would cost me an opportunity to grow my allowance. Besides sliding pamphlets under each door, Beauty and I would walk around the neighbourhood handing out the pamphlets. Most students would smile and ask, 'When can you fetch my laundry?' This brought great joy to me because I felt this was the beginning of my first formal business. At least, that's what I thought.

My first order came in. It arrived via a WhatsApp message. The customer supplied me with his details and I collected the washing. From that first order, the business grew to the point where Beauty and I could not meet the demand. And because of my saving habits, I had enough money to hire more washers and cleaners. I put an advert online, collected CVs and interviewed people. I had little experience in recruitment so I went online and I looked for interview templates. I realised that many women in Johannesburg would avail their services as cleaners. It's tough to find a job in Jozi, and these women had families to feed. I could have taken any one of them but I needed to ensure that they were trustworthy in order to avoid theft in the rooms that they cleaned.

My business operated in a very simplistic manner. I measured the square metres of each type of apartment in the Milpark Mews complex and I constructed my pricing structure as follows: R70 for a bachelor flat, R90 for a one-bedroom flat and R110 for a two-bedroom flat. These rates were based on the fact that a cleaner could clean approximately three rooms per day. I would then take 20%, and 80% went to the cleaner.

As time went by people started asking Beauty questions about my pricing structure, and she felt that the 20% I was taking was too much. With the business growing at a fast rate, I soon encountered a challenge. Beauty had made arrangements with other people in the building to clean their apartments in her personal capacity, offering her more money than she was making with me.

This felt like high school all over again. Another person was taking advantage of my trust.

I had to move on and find someone else who would take on her duties. So I hired Flora, who differed from Beauty in many ways. First of all, she wasn't very outspoken, meaning that she would arrive at an apartment and go about her business without making too much conversation. She would not create a space where the tenants felt they could solicit her services. But Flora and I established trust between us and we worked well together.

The fear of being humiliated is one I overcame quite fast as an entrepreneur because we live in a world that takes pleasure in an individual's failure more than in his success.

The business expanded to other buildings in and around the Auckland Park area. I gave a lot of thought to how this lucrative business could continue. So I went on with the cleaning aspect of the business and stopped the laundry service. I closed it down because someone had seen my pamphlets and had hijacked my customers from me single-handedly. Understandably so, because he was offering the same service that I offered, but at a cheaper price. This was enough to appeal to the students.

We continued with the cleaning business, but that did not exist without its own set of challenges. The service industry relies on working with people, and people are complex. I would receive petty complaints like: 'There is a streak on my window ...' And because I was inexperienced, I knew little about managing customer complaints. I would respond: 'So wipe it off with a tissue!' and this left me with very unhappy customers.

You might be wondering about how I managed my studies amid all the chaos of running my business. I had befriended a group of diligent students. They were smart and focused, and so I asked them to take down lecture notes for me during class if I couldn't make it so that they could share these with me. This did not come without its own set of challenges; my friends would get annoyed with me, and I had to bribe them with lunch or a small fee to continue. They knew I was making money from my little business, and they also knew that I needed their help with the study notes – so they exploited me in my time of need.

The fear of being humiliated is one I overcame quite fast as an entrepreneur because we live in a world that takes pleasure in an individual's failure more than in his success. This is a stumbling block I constantly faced in my laundry and cleaning business, and getting over it was a pivotal step in my success. The fear of humiliation often stifles businesses. I make it seem simple to overcome, but as a young person, doing people's laundry and cleaning their apartments is not as glamorous as the business ventures we often fantasise about. Various incidents occurred where I was ridiculed for running a laundry and cleaning business. Once people discovered I was the person behind it, I would encounter different reactions.

One day, I was at the student gym working out and another student attempted to humiliate me by asking: 'When will you pick up my washing, laundry man?' Everyone at the gym was expecting a response from me. They were waiting for retaliation, but I responded calmly and professionally, 'When can I come and pick it up?' And he said: 'Today.' Of course, I was a little embarrassed but proud that I could think on my feet and respond to the situation swiftly. His nasty remark didn't have the desired effect! Instead, other students were in awe of me. They wondered how I juggled both my studies and my laundry business. This incident was a reinforcement of the fact that expanding my business and making a profit was more important than what people thought of me.

A culture of saving definitely pays off in the future.

I had been operating for several months, and a few people were stunned that I wasn't registered with CIPC, nor did I have a business bank account. I was advised to register my business. There was still a lot to do and a lot that I needed to know. I researched how to do this, and within a matter of days I registered the business, then opened a bank account.

Toward the end of my first year, I noticed a vast difference between myself and my peers, because partying, smoking and drinking was a norm among them. While they would party, I would pick up Flora from the train station so we could head to our next job. This paid off for me because the business grew, and we cleaned large office buildings in Johannesburg's bustling Braamfontein district. But soon enough, the service industry wore me down; complaints from petty customers became overwhelming. I lost passion in the business, so I chose to look into new income streams. I was proud of my achievements, and the most important lesson I learned is: 'It can be done!'

I learned a great deal from my first faltering steps as a businessman. And the first piece of wisdom concerned lifestyle. For example, some youngsters spend all their money on partying, alcohol and ridiculously expensive clothes. I preferred to keep some of the money and find ways to make it grow. Instead of buying lunch like most students, I packed a lunch and continued to save my own money. I would also refrain from activities that would have lowered my bank balance. I learned how to save, and when I started my new business I had some capital. It's very important to save money with a clear vision in mind – not just aimlessly. Nowadays, and in our harsh economy, most people find it tough to save. But a culture of saving definitely pays off in the future. Many young people have a lot of responsibilities, along with different money and lifestyle needs. A good budgeting plan can go a long way. Of course, people argue that they don't have anything left to save after they've paid all the bills. But luxuries can sometimes be sacrificed for the sake of a better future. There were things that I had to go without in order to earn the things that I wanted. I liked to call it 'compromising with my temptations'. But it's okay to spoil yourself once in a while, so long as it's in moderation.

Personal sacrifices show how dedicated you are to your own business. And this is important when you're looking for funding, because it's rare to find someone willing to fund your business idea 100%. The reality is this: people don't really care about your dreams as much as you do. At best, they can listen and sympathise and maybe give some advice, but they will never give as much as you do. It's important to save from a young age because it creates an important culture of being invested in the future.

Growing up, I had been curious about the financial status of people around us in Venda, because wealthy people would die but then their children would struggle. My parents told me why: it was usually because the children were not taught how to save their money. When you are so used to being spoon fed and taken care of, you get lost once the director and direction is taken away. It is important to grasp the concept of independence and use it every single chance you get. Spending money is easier than saving it – there's no debate about it. But having money is better than having nothing. My advice is simple: 'Save what you can, you will never regret it!'

It doesn't have to be insane amounts of cash, and it need not affect your lifestyle negatively. It can just be a habit that you develop. I can proudly say that the capital I used for my first business came from the savings that I made in high school and the small sacrifices I made every single day when I decided to go without something.

Most of the time, entrepreneurs feel they need funding from big corporations to get started. Yet a simple approach to fulfilling a need can spark a successful business. I recognised a need within my community, and I came up with the best solution that I could conjure up at the time, given my limited experience. As I pursued this service, I ensured that I had the basics to run a laundry and cleaning business – a washing machine and a lady who cleaned.

In more formal environments, my idea would be referred to as a MVP, a Minimal Viable Product. These have been used by some of the greatest entrepreneurs of all time, including Elon Musk and Steve Jobs. Going to market with an MVP is what you need, and as the demand grows, so does the product or service.

In those early stages of my business, I cultivated my style of interviewing people and used my instincts to determine their trustworthiness. I also tried cross checking references. To date, I have conducted over 1000 recruitment interviews without consulting a third party. And from these interviews I have learned to detect whether a person is the right fit for a position. As an entrepreneur, it's important to hone basic skills such as interviewing people, as they are the cornerstone of your business, and you can find ways to identify people who are suited to your requirements.

I learned the art of constant innovation by being resilient and seeking solutions, every step of the way. I faced each stumbling block with the determination to grow my business.

Gathering data in the interview process was also pivotal in hiring cleaners for my small business in order to assess competence and trustworthiness.

For small businesses, experience creates an opportunity to learn, and each failure is a lesson that moulds a business person into a strong individual able to conduct business with dignity. At times, being excited about the business can cause an oversight in the most basic areas, particularly structural requirements such as paperwork, including contracts and other agreements. A paper trail protects all parties when disputes take place, and contracts ensure that each party operates within certain parameters. With Beauty, I assumed that a contract was not needed because we worked well together, but a valuable lesson revealed itself: my employees needed contracts to operate according to my expectations. In business, you will often find people like Beauty who will try find a way around the system you have put in place, in order to uplift themselves. It's your responsibility as owner to know how to handle these fallouts.

When it came to the structural limitation of my business, I learned the art of constant innovation by being resilient and seeking solutions, every step of the way. I faced each stumbling block with the determination to grow my business. I feel that this is an important trait for all entrepreneurs because you need to be open to change and adapt to circumstances. It is important to pay attention to detail and notice the gaps where you can continue your business and make revenue. Being an entrepreneur is realising the task at hand and fulfilling it. When I faced the constraint of my business not being able to continue in my apartment; I ensured that as long as my activities were not of a criminal nature and did not harm others – I could pursue this laundry business with success. During that time, I realised that I had it in me to do whatever it takes to keep my business going, without relying on help from a funder. I was becoming independent.

I realised that a key element in the service industry is enjoying the act of interacting with customers. The service industry is the most challenging because people's personalities differ and they all have different demands, so passion goes a long way. Above all, I had no passion for this business and it did not make sense for me to continue with such an enterprise. I realised that in future I would be an unhappy boss, which would then result in an unhappy workforce.

My laundry and cleaning business gave me a lot of insight into building a successful business. Although it's no longer in existence, it formed the flourishing businesses I run today, because I learned the core principles of entrepreneurship. Furthermore, it's easy to get caught up in making money, rather than focusing on what you're actually about, because that's where the key to building a successful business lies. In this day and age, ideas are easily plagiarised or even dressed up to paraphrase your original concept. Innovation is key, and an MVP can give you an idea of what is required in the market, how to improve on the product and how to attract potential investors. It is certainly possible to develop an MVP while holding down your job or completing your degree.

Such a project can provide you with pivotal information about the market you operate within, and you get to know your customer base on a small scale. An MVP is much like in-depth research into how you can make your product or service better, and it's what ensures that you get profits because your product or service accommodates and understands the market it operates within. Investors actively seek a Return on Investment (ROI), and this is why it's important to understand the value of your company, and the idea you have. This creates room for negotiation. Clients play a pivotal role in developing your business because they determine its true value by participating in an exchange with you, and so these statistics show an investor how much your product is actually worth.

Statistics show that 90% of enterprises fail because they take time to yield returns. Sometimes businesses may take up to three years to break even, and this is when entrepreneurs begin to give up. It's important to start small and grow from being just a MVP into a successful enterprise. It is important to cultivate an awareness of where you stand as an individual and grow from that point. You need to be patient, balance your time and sacrifice what you feel won't benefit the future of your business.

At that age, given peer pressure and the urge to fit in, I learned that in business, there is little room for your pride; what's needed in business are fresh ideas, innovation and making the necessary sacrifices to succeed. So being known as Mpho, the guy who does laundry, didn't bother me because my heart was set on becoming a successful businessman.

At that point in time, the laundry and cleaning businesses were the only things that I knew, so I milked the cow the best way I could. I came up with viable and implementable strategies on how to continue growing the business and I focused less on what people thought of me. My focus shifted to actively growing, formalising and expanding my business.

Chapter Four tells the story of my arrival at university and how I started a laundry and cleaning business. I took many false steps along the way and learned much from my failures. I already knew the vital importance of saving. And I gathered much practical business savvy, on top of the theoretical background my grandparents and parents had given me. This was the real nitty-gritty of business: identifying a need and offering to meet it, using savings as capital to establish a Minimal Viable Project. My project was tiny, but capable of expansion. In those days I managed to think fast and survive, despite setbacks such as Beauty's disloyalty. I learned to tough it out when students mocked me and made lifestyle sacrifices. I learned a lot about operating a business: the sacrifices in lifestyle that bring independence, the need for one's own self-generated capital. I learned the value of starting small, in a business with growth potential, and the constant innovation that got me over obstacles such as competition. And I also learned lessons in trust, as I interviewed job applicants. But the biggest lesson to be drawn from this chapter is: it can be done.

CHAPTER FOUR: KEY LESSONS

1. Find out what people need, and if they're willing to pay for that need to be met. Then provide the service required, using savings as capital, as I did when I bought the washing machine.

2. Be inquisitive and passionate about the business you're in. Ask questions, find out what people say and think. Be on the lookout for changes, and remember that a business must adapt or die in response. I managed to be flexible as I met a growing demand.

3. Start with what you have, then expand. But first make sure that the possibility for growth is there, as I did when the cleaning business expanded into office blocks.

4. A challenge is also an opportunity. I experienced competition from a business which undercut my prices, which led to a whole new field of endeavour. See Chapter Five.

5. Develop this attitude: it can be done. Even when the task seems daunting, keep trying, as I did when I registered my business and began to exceed my own expectations.

FIVE

Fail, learn – continue!

After closing my cleaning service, I began a quest for optimal profits with minimal efforts. I met a lady named Awe who sold Herbalife products, for managing weight loss and nutrition. I became interested in joining Awe on this venture because she was making a lot of money. With network marketing, people focus narrowly on selling the prospect of success. I was good at this, so I was confident that I would certainly make money selling Herbalife.

Within no time I realised that selling these products was very difficult! People didn't easily buy into what I was selling, so I decided to sell the benefits of the products. In those years I was chubby, so I gave the products a test run and marketed the benefits using myself as an example. I lost the weight, but despite this effort, I still struggled to lock down clients and this was a source of great frustration. Awe was successful in her marketing strategy as it was social at heart. She was active on Facebook and would lure clients by selling the benefits on her social media profiles. Then she would invite people to Shake Parties to taste and buy the products. Awe's strategy worked for her because she's an extrovert. But I'm an introvert, so I soon lost interest in Herbalife.

Amway showed me that within a network marketing scheme, one can remain at the bottom of the food chain for a long time.

My quest for passive income continued, and I came across another network marketing group, Amway. This was another international company which uses multi-level marketing to sell health, beauty, and home care products. Again, I was sold on the dream and I joined them. We would create events around the products selling the benefits of Amway. These events attracted people, but I still struggled to make recruits. I even tried to recruit my parents, who declined with the utmost respect. Amway showed me that within a network marketing scheme, one can remain at the bottom of the food chain for a long time. That is why I left Amway. I needed something new, and I needed something different. I couldn't let my failure with Amway determine my next move. I had to carry on and take the failure as another opportunity to learn and grow.

Having an idea for a new business venture is one thing, but having the guts and the time to implement your idea is another. As I interacted with the business world and business people, I spotted a mistake that's often made. And that is to quit your current job or studies to pursue a business idea. In business, passion and bravery go hand-in-hand, but sensibility and time management are the keys to success. I started my business while I was still a student because I wanted to have an option once I completed my studies. I wanted to ensure that I had something to fall back on, should I not find a job in my field of study. My parents were very clear that they would only support me to a certain point – because I was expected to complete my studies, find a job and support myself. So I didn't tell them about the business I was running while simultaneously applying myself to my studies. I could not tell the people who inspired me the most in the first place about how I was following in their footsteps. These small failures were moulding me into the person that I am today. When you think about your business, what runs through your mind? Don't just think of the end result but about the building blocks as well: your business plan, your team, your strategies. Break down your thoughts into building blocks that will lead to your end result.

When you look at what you're trying to build, look at it from the end but always start from the beginning. Envision what you want to achieve, then figure out ways to get to it. In the building process you'll come across unforeseen changes and you just have to accept them as they come. If you stick to a static and rigid mentality, chances are you won't go far because the business world is ever evolving and things change every day.

It's important to adopt a flexible mindset if you're going to make it, because certain things will force you to change your route, and if you're not flexible enough you just might give up. Step into your business with a flexible mentality and be ready to solve whatever challenge comes your way. Be a problem solver who always thinks of new ways of tackling challenges. And most importantly – be innovative. You also need to adopt a mentality that doesn't give up because you are sure to encounter serious hurdles. Instead of being overwhelmed by problems you must always think like a winner.

Seeking advice and reading books helps shape your mentality. You become a resourceful thinker and with time your mentality broadens and doesn't limit you. Get into the habit of reading, and don't seek validation from opinions – but rather from research. One person's opinion cannot be your deciding vote. You also need to broaden your perspective and rely on factual information instead of opinions and anecdotes.

Businesses encounter various challenges in the initial growth stages which often lead to financial constraints. If you have a business idea, go out and implement it. If you fail, fail quickly, learn from it and improve. Instead of sitting idly waiting for funding, rather take the initiative and fail if you are going to fail. This concept will eliminate any fears that the business might not work. Start and fail. And then in that failure, learn why it did not work out, find a solution, integrate it and continue with your business.

Failure makes you a stronger person and gives you an opportunity to improve. After failure you bounce back as a wiser and more knowledgeable business person.

This whole concept acknowledges that failure is almost always inevitable. So instead of quitting, explore the market more, find out what is wrong with your product or service, fix it and continue. Your product should always be suitable for consumers. Most entrepreneurs paint pictures of their products and services in their minds that appear brilliant to them. But when they take them to the market, the market rejects what's on offer, or simply doesn't relate to it. It is important that you do market research, test your idea, implement it and see how the market receives it. Do not let an idea incubate in your mind.

One easy way of doing this is through a website landing page. Create a page where people can learn all they need to know about your product or service. Simply put, a landing page is a platform where you get to test the market, simulating what you'll be selling. Visitors will be able to look and leave their feedback. This will give you an indication of how people will receive the actual offering. And then you'll know whether to pursue it or not. Instead of sitting on an idea and cultivating it only in your mind, rather get up and do something. Take action, test the market, fail fast and pick yourself up. The sequence of fail, learn and continue will enable you to build a polished product.

Chapter Five is all about how failure makes you a stronger person and gives you an opportunity to improve. After failure you bounce back as a wiser and more knowledgeable business person. This was one thing I learned through my attempts to start businesses. One of the clearest lessons for me was this: failure is an important ingredient of success. You need to stretch yourself as an entrepreneur, because if you don't then you're not growing, and you're never going to know your full strength. There is no room for growth in playing it safe and doing what has been done before. Extend yourself and realise your full potential.

As we navigate business, we realise that investor funding is not that easy to come by. Instead of waiting for an investor, I invested my time in growing myself. My friends would often joke that I was like a ghost because I wasn't even on social media. At that point, I would spend all my time working on different ways of becoming wealthy. These days, I find that people are stunned when I advise them to keep their jobs or continue their studies while they start a new venture. A lawyer at entry level once approached me and asked: 'I work from 9 am right up until 6 pm! How do you think I can find the time to focus on business?' I simply asked him: 'What are weekends for?'

Often, as in my personal experience, entrepreneurs fund their own ventures and strain can occur if an individual has no supplementary income. In my opinion, you should keep your job and pursue business because this creates room to earn an income and grow your passion. A fundamental contributor to my success was my ability to focus on two things at once: education and my business.

Sacrifice is necessary in the early stages of an enterprise. All along my journey I was combining study with entrepreneurship, and I learned the importance of making valuable sacrifices. This includes time management, and the delay of pleasures. Focusing on your business instead of going to a party will surely pay off. A business is similar to being in a relationship, because it's a constant negotiation of time, energy and dedication to make it grow and flourish. Nobody likes to experience failure, as I did with Herbalife and Amway. When this is accompanied by financial strain, an entrepreneur may give up and even decide to never embark on another business. I firmly believe that it is possible to use the spare hours in your day and weekend to implement an idea. An idea on its own is rarely enough to quit your job for, so stay in school and don't quit your job until there comes a point when your business is clearly being hindered by your job, and yields enough profits to cover your expenses.

CHAPTER FIVE: KEY LESSONS

1. Don't be afraid of failure. It can be a bitter and humbling experience, but it is also a new beginning and a source of valuable experience. Failure is more common in business than most people imagine and nothing to be ashamed of.

2. Treat each failure as a learning experience. The young entrepreneur learns much about business and the ways of the world through failure. If an investment opportunity seems too good to be true, it's probably a scam.

3. Young entrepreneurs learn personal lessons from failure, invaluable self knowledge about talents, attitudes, weaknesses and strong points. I was temperamentally unsuited to the kind of salesmanship that is required in businesses such as Amway and Herbalife.

4. Failure makes you a stronger person and leads into new and more promising paths in life. Be proactive in the face of constant change, keep asking: 'What if ...'

5. Use the time you have. There is always a method to combine study or a day job with the beginning of a new enterprise which you have dreamed up. But don't give up the bread-and-butter income until the new idea is covering costs.

SIX

Stokvel to Bitcoin

At university, I could look back on an interesting life. I had grown up in a family that was very business oriented. From a young age I had been preoccupied with the idea of wealth and was determined to become successful. By the time I was in second year, I had already established my own cleaning business, and had learned that network marketing schemes such as Herbalife and Amway did not suit my character. So I explored social media, using this transparent platform to find out how people were making money on a daily basis. I participated and observed the conversations. And the first thing I noticed was a growing presence of stokvels on social media. I made contact with a woman who was part of a stokvel club and, at first glance, I suspected she may have been a part of a Ponzi scheme, which I already knew was one of the oldest frauds in the modern world.

The stokvel model appealed to me. Any South African is familiar with the concept of a stokvel – an invitation-only club where people rotate savings and credit on a regular basis. There are different types of stokvels, with the most popular being the contribution model. A lot of innovation has taken place over the years. There are at least eight types of stokvels and more than 800 000 in existence in South Africa.

The stokvel has always functioned as a support system for women in black communities. Stokvels originated from the need to help each other with what you have – in an ongoing exchange.

My mother was a member of stokvels which operated differently. A group of ladies would gather rotationally at members' houses on a monthly basis. The hostess was required to prepare beverages and food, including scones, and a traditional 'Sunday meal'. The group would then start off with a song and short prayer. Then they would open their books to review monies contributed and monies owed to the group as well as expenses such as funerals and weddings. Contributions to baby showers were considered donations to fellow members. These were made as a way of appreciating the people's membership in their stokvel. The members would discuss the next event and what their donation would be toward it.

Members of my mother's stokvel would be seen at these events, dressed in the stokvel uniform, ready to assist where they were needed, from peeling vegetables to ensuring that the function went according to plan. The stokvel has always functioned as a support system for women in black communities. We have always showed up to assist in other members' homes during important ceremonies such as weddings and funerals. Because it's meant to be a shared effort by the community to make the event a success. Africans have always believed in sharing such responsibilities, and this is encapsulated in the spirit of ubuntu. Stokvels originated from the need to help each other with what you have – in an ongoing exchange.

The stokvel I came across on Facebook was an investment group which operated differently from the traditional contribution-based stokvel. One of the claims made on the page was that you could get up to 20% return per month on your investment. I was intrigued. The comments on the page were littered with testimonials. I was drawn to the possibility of passive income but I wasn't naive about it so I was very cautious when I approached the woman who managed the page. Their meetings were held in Johannesburg's township, Soweto. I attended a meeting, which was jam-packed with older women wearing T-shirts with 'Kipi' printed on them.

Much as in a traditional stokvel, the women started off with a song, followed by a prayer. Then a woman stood up and gave a presentation, explaining how the scheme worked for newcomers like myself. The women wore expressions of secret gloating on their faces, and this strange new stokvel became even more alluring. Clearly Kipi was working for them. But it was incomprehensible to a newcomer like myself. Throughout the meeting, the existing members chanted statements such as: 'Kipi! Our Saviour!' The crowd became ecstatic as the presentation went on. And we, the potential recruits, were even more curious about the scheme. Clearly it was creating money for its members, at least that's what their behaviour indicated.

I had seen many communities rally around wealth, but this particular community had cultivated a unique sense of ubuntu. There was a captivating sense of unity among the members because the scheme had given them the hope of financial freedom. The presentation itself differed from most sales presentations because you often feel manipulated into buying something you don't necessarily need or want. Here, a lifestyle was being marketed. The possibilities seemed endless and the benefits seemed worthwhile. It was more than a sales pitch for new recruits – it had the relaxed feeling of a family gathering. The community members clearly cared for each other and were reaping serious benefits from this entity. The most significant thing I noticed with these women was how comfortable they felt with each other and with Kipi.

In this particular stokvel, the scheme was online based. My curiosity was piqued, but I remained quite sceptical. Yet I was impressed by these women who were clearly making the passive income I was after. They also came across as mature and seemed to know what they were doing. The room was filled with respectable, hardworking people such as lawyers, teachers and other professionals who had found this stokvel online. Up to this point, in my understanding, stokvels did not exist online. My concept of a stokvel was a group of people who deposited money into a joint account entrusted to the most trustworthy members.

The model of stokvels had clearly evolved with technology. I had grown up watching my mother participating in them, so I was accustomed to a structure where members contributed a fixed amount of money to a common pool monthly and then each member would receive the lump sum on a rotational basis, and they were free to use the money for any purpose. The model of the stokvel clearly needed to evolve because this particular model did not respond well to inflation. The Rand devalues with time, and the money does not accumulate any interest.

Kipi was different. The zeal these women had for what they were doing was impressive, to say the least. They gave moving testimonials on how they had achieved their dreams and made money through investing online. Women stood up and spoke about how they had put their children through university using money from Kipi. One said she'd paid for her husband's funeral. This left questions in my mind about how stokvel money could actually help to pay off something big. I asked myself: Does she mean the money came from the stokvel – or did she mean that this was the money she reaped after the savings period? In the case of the funeral, I assumed that she meant the club contributed to the cost of the funeral, as most people in African communities do when a family member passes away.

The women at that Soweto gathering would conclude their testimonials by proclaiming: 'Kipi, we love you!' One went to the extent of saying: 'I will die for Kipi', because the money she invested had grown to a point where she could build herself a house. I was astonished, I wanted to know more about how this particular stokvel went about paying for such large expenses in these people's lives. I needed to understand why these women would go to the extent of proclaiming that they would *die* for this online stokvel.

At the end of the moving presentation, the main speaker drilled into our minds that we must recruit more people to join. In the room, most members sat next to someone like me who was recently recruited or being convinced to join. This was when I grew sceptical, convinced that this was clearly a Ponzi scheme. As the main speaker broke down how Kipi worked, it became evident that money was generated from new members' fees. It was a sketchy system that relied solely on trust. The new recruits contributed to pay-outs for existing members, but new recruits had no guarantee that the favour would be returned.

Despite my scepticism, the testimonials reverberated in my mind and I felt that something worthwhile might materialise from this. Kipi was established in Russia in 1995. The scheme had operated in over 80 countries including South Africa, where it was established in 2013, the year I discovered it. To get started, you needed to create an account on the website, then add your dream along with the money you were able to donate. Your initial donation earned you a daily interest of 0.6% while you helped another user achieve their goal. The donation allowed your balance to grow, and as other members joined and donated, you would notice your progress line improving until you had enough for others to donate and make your dream a reality.

At the core of Kipi, also known as MyDeposit247, was a networking model to help a community of people reach their financial goals. The platform was highly accessible, and it cultivated a community of people who became loyal advocates. I understood the loyalty that people had towards Kipi because many South Africans live just above the poverty line, and the scheme offered people an opportunity to earn high returns on their investments. Here is an example of how it worked: You would invest (donate) a minimum of R200. If you wanted R4000 from your R200, you would get it after 16 months. The R4000 would then be referred to as a *Dream*. An additional way to earn more money was to invite other people to join and thereby earn a percentage of the joining fee. I was interested in making ZAR2 million; one member testified that she initially invested ZAR100 000 and got ZAR2 million in less than two years. This story gave me hope that my dream would come to fruition.

I started off by investing small amounts, watching them grow and quickly withdrawing them. I then moved on to a bigger amount and invested R2000 from my savings in the hope of getting R20 000 after one year. I then decided that I would work toward a dream of R200 000, so I invested R20 000 that I had won in a high school raffle. I witnessed the scheme growing at an exponential rate because of the referral system; each time a new member joined, the recruiter earned money. With time, I grew close to the women, as I attended more meetings. Younger people started to join. Despite the sense of community I had built with the women in the club, the founder remained a mystery to most of us, and I grew increasingly concerned about this. Passive income is often the selling point of pyramid schemes, because early adopters earn high amounts of money for minimal effort. Our banks offer low interest rates, so when Ponzi schemes hit our shores people signed up at a fast rate.

But the membership started dwindling when a new investment scheme emerged, known as MMM. Instead of Kipi's 0.6% interest daily, MMM promised 30% compounded per month. Then Kipi introduced a subscription fee that was to be paid only in Bitcoin (0.2 BTC). At the time no one knew what Bitcoin was and I knew nothing about cryptocurrencies. The emails sent out to members said their subscriptions would be cancelled if these fees were not paid. I grew increasingly concerned because my dream of R200 000 was left with 10 months to mature and still had a year before my ZAR2 million dream was scheduled to mature.

At the meeting following the announcement, people were perplexed as to what Bitcoin was and how to pay this subscription. No one knew how they could acquire Bitcoin, yet without this cryptic coin they were at risk of losing their hard-earned money. The whole community was in distress and the leader of our group assured members that they would find a way to buy Bitcoin to pay for subscriptions. The members were in a frenzy. As exciting as it was to be part of an international scheme, there was a downside when it came to understanding certain aspects of the technology they were using.

The confusion created panic, and an inevitable breakdown was looming as the community tried to wrap its head around this new problem of acquiring Bitcoin. Although the stokvel was primarily made up of older people, even younger people like myself didn't understand what this Bitcoin was and how it worked. The risk of losing my money motivated me to find out more, how to get it and how it worked. I became even more determined to find a way to help myself and the rest of the community by paying for our subscriptions as per requirement.

Any situation that involves money is accompanied by greed.

I wanted to know who had sent the email stating that we needed to pay the subscription fee. That's when I started looking for clues on how to get to the bottom of the scheme. The women were preoccupied with finding out how to acquire Bitcoin but I briefly diverted their focus to the people behind Kipi. I grew increasingly curious about the founder and I felt it was important to find out. When I asked the women whether they knew who had started Kipi, I hit a dead end and was very frustrated. As we looked into this matter, one woman exclaimed, 'I hope this doesn't pan out the way Defencex did.'

I was curious about Defencex, and discovered that prior to Kipi, the same group of women were involved in a scheme known as Defencex – led by the controversial Chris Walker – which subsequently collapsed. Defencex offered a daily interest of 2%, but a lot of people ended up losing their money. After Walker's accounts were frozen by the Reserve Bank, he told his followers to join Kipi and recover their lost money. There was some speculation that he was also behind the new scheme. As it began to fall apart, the women grew understandably concerned.

At some point I thought it might be as easy as sending an email to find out the information. Kipi was generally prompt when it came to emails regarding technical support, so I made the assumption that someone would get back to me just as fast if I asked who owned the company. I never got a response.

I learned a vital lesson about Ponzi schemes: those who invested their monies in the beginning got it back with the promised interest and those who joined later were likely to lose their money.

Following the subscription issue, Kipi experienced a hacking scandal, and people could not withdraw their money. Furthermore, the victims began to question why the subscription fee was going up and down. I realised that it was the actual cryptocurrency that was fluctuating. And although quite volatile, I noted that its general trend was a steady increase. But the volatility of Bitcoin made it harder to recruit new members into Kipi. Subscriptions were cancelled if members failed to submit the payment of 0.2 BTC. And soon enough, I realised that my R20 000 Dream had turned into a nightmare. I was never going to get my money back.

Kipi finally crashed and I had to consider ways to recover my money. I made several attempts to mobilise members to open a court case against the founders of Kipi, but we had no idea how to trace them. I also realised that this was a futile attempt at justice because each person was recruited by another, and it was an endless chain leading to nowhere. I conducted further research and hit countless dead ends. I even contacted an IT expert to trace the servers and he simply told me that they were 'in the cloud'. Furthermore, the fact that Bitcoin was used as a mode of payment left us clueless as to who was behind this scheme. When I approached the members, most of them told me that they got involved on the understanding that there were risks involved in joining, so they had made peace with losing their money.

Finally, I too had made peace with losing my money and, within a few weeks, other members called me and told me about a new investment opportunity from a company based in Braamfontein called Melrose Property Fund, which apparently invested specifically in the up-market suburb of Melrose. This company, on Juta Street, seemed legitimate and offered high returns; unlike Kipi, it was more than a simple website – they had offices! I took this as a good sign. I also saw certificates on the wall, so I was convinced that everything was above board and I would not fall victim again.

Furthermore, there were positive testimonials from people I met in the course of my research into how the company made money from the investments. And so I was sold. I was promised high returns on the amount I would invest. The more I invested, the more money I stood to make – so I signed a contract and invested all the money I had. I left their offices feeling assured that I had found a new way to make passive income. I scraped together all I could, which amounted to some R7000, and deposited the money. Then I had to wait two weeks for it to mature.

The prospect of my money growing excited me. I was already seeing my dreams taking shape and I was excited that for the first time, I could tell my parents about my efforts and they would be so proud of the results. The two-week mark had come and I went to collect my money. I returned to the offices and the downstairs receptionist informed me that the company had left the building. In disbelief, I attempted to trace their whereabouts, and this led me to yet another dead end. I had to come to terms with the fact I had lost money – once again. I was completely broke. I couldn't go to my parents and ask for money without telling them what I had done with all my other money. I was depressed because I now felt I could never meet any of my lifestyle needs.

One of the most pivotal lessons I gained from my experience with Kipi was that whoever created the concept had good intentions. It consisted of people passing money around from one person to the next, but any situation that involves money is accompanied by greed. For a long time, I grappled with what could have caused the collapse and I came to a few conclusions. The owner possibly became too greedy. That was probably why he or she had introduced the Bitcoin payment system – to yield more profits. In addition, this person was able to access funds and paying in Bitcoin presented limitations to a large proportion of the Kipi community, which meant the owner would keep the money of those who could not access Bitcoin. Members started to suspect that the hacking scandal was an inside job because the people who established it were not happy with the direction things were going. Another possibility was that members were reaping serious benefits from Kipi, and this could have alarmed the owners.

Although Kipi did not work out, it left me exploring the possibilities of Bitcoin and how possible it was to transfer it anonymously. Unlike a bank account, Bitcoin does not disclose the person who receives money, and this is a double-edged sword. Because in the case of Ponzi schemes it means that you will never be able to locate and recover your money.

During this time, although I was not the only person who fell victim to Ponzi and pyramid schemes, I learned the hard way that the prospect of easy money is often accompanied by great risk, and great loss.

I learned a vital lesson about Ponzi schemes: those who invested their monies in the beginning got it back with the promised interest and those who joined later were likely to lose their money. In both my previous incidents, I was one of the last people to join the schemes and subsequently lost my money.

In Chapter Six, I tell the sad story of my naive younger self, who fell for various get-rich-quick schemes, which outwardly resembled the familiar stokvels my mother had joined in the rural areas of Venda. But the resemblance was superficial; Kipi had no bank accounts or offices, only an enticing website. Early adopters collected huge passive incomes financed by the innocents at the end of the queue. This was the principle behind the dying Kipi and other Ponzi scams such as Melrose Property Fund. But the one shining light in Chapter Six is my discovery of Bitcoin. It was my destiny, but I didn't know that yet.

CHAPTER SIX: KEY LESSONS

1. There are more scams in the world than genuine investment opportunities.
2. Don't be greedy, look for a fair return. Low-risk investments such as my mother's stokvel savings take time to grow and require patience.
3. The only way to play Ponzi is to get in and out at a very early stage. If you have no idea how long the scam has been running, you're ripe for a rip-off. I remember my tears after Melrose.
4. Great profit only comes as a result of great risk. This applies to legitimate business.
5. Base investments on careful research, and take nothing at face value. When you listen to anyone describing an investment scheme, ask yourself: does it sound too good to be true, or defy the rules of simple arithmetic? If so, walk away.

SEVEN

Taking the wrong types of risks

Every entrepreneur goes through a phase when he or she reaches the point that they have been successful enough to become so hungry for more that they might go into some or other venture without careful evaluation of the situation first. Before I mastered Bitcoin and made some money, I was determined to explore and conquer other business opportunities. This, what I like to call, crazy phase begins with the idea that you are capable of making money in any way. You are overcome by the adrenalin of success, and you want to achieve more. I believed that stumbling across Bitcoin was the beginning of my success as an entrepreneur, so I actively pursued new ventures and went through a wide array of potential quick ways to make money.

A new Ponzi scheme made its way to my ears. I was told about a scheme called MMM which promised up to 30% return on investments in 30 days. I gave this some thought and concluded that this scheme would close down soon, so the plan was to ride the wave before it collapsed. During the first few weeks, I invested small amounts of money, watched them grow and withdrew them like I did with Kipi. MMM's 30% returns made it very popular quite quickly.

A while back, my mother had opened a savings account for me with Old Mutual. I visited the offices in Johannesburg to withdraw my savings, which amounted to R10 000. I knew this was an immense risk after being burned twice, but after seven days my money had grown by 7% so I withdrew it. I walked away with R10 700. It was a small but quick profit and decided I would no longer get involved in Ponzi schemes. I saved my cash and continued to muse on other ways to make money.

Because I was in my crazy phase and taking the wrong types of risks, I came across and was taken in by an email advertising how people can make money through betting in sports on an American website called Sports Cash Betting. Of course, the website was littered with testimonials and the owner promised to guide users through the process. I followed the subscription process, and this was exciting for me because the prospect of easy money is appealing to most people. The betting was based on the NFL baseball games in America; and the experts over at Sports Cash Betting would recommend which team to bet on, and in the first few instances, I won. The experts seemed like trustworthy sports analysts who would advise me on what to bet on, and each bet was based on what they said. They were often right, but sometimes they would be wrong, and the advice they gave us was to bet double the next day so you could make that money back.

I then started to explore new betting systems; in my perspective I could gamble conservatively and do it responsibly in order to make money. I felt that I could turn it into a business opportunity.

My idea of betting responsibly failed dismally and I was unable to sustain it due to the fact that gambling is a game of chance.

Predictably, I started to lose money at a rapid pace in sports, because sports are based on human nature, and human nature is erratic, and the predictors were beginning to make more and more errors, which led to a loss of some hard-earned money.

I then decided to move onto a betting system that was based less on human nature and more reliant on an algorithm, or so I thought. So I began betting on the UK High-Low Lottery. For example: US Powerball is a 59-ball guess range lottery. Low numbers are in the range 1 to 29; high numbers are in the range 30 to 59.

As I delved into betting, my idea of betting responsibly failed dismally and I was unable to sustain it due to the fact that gambling is a game of chance, and I had therefore taken the wrong type of risk by getting into gambling. Winning is not always guaranteed, and so I ended up losing more money than I won. I soon realised that volatility did not always translate to profitability. In addition, the people who gamble and bet online, not many of them make money. The companies that take the bets make the most money, so gambling is rarely designed to profit the gambler.

I discovered a form of trading known as binary trading. In the past few years this form of trading has grown in popularity, and people attest to its effectiveness. In a nutshell, Binary Trading is basically a matter of predicting whether a market in the US dollar or Chinese yuan is going up or down. You win if your prediction is right. In my view, binary trading mimics gambling, although it is regulated, and your predictions are more practical because they are based on research.

This prompted me to study the market. I started conducting research in the initial phase, but my passion for binary trading slowly dwindled with time. This again was a symptom of being stuck in the crazy phase that every entrepreneur goes through. Moreover, each time I lost a trade, I would suffer from depression and sadness. I had little passion for it, and so I left the binary trading world while I still had my money.

As I continued to search for avenues of passive income, I came across a friend who told me about forex trading and presented this as highly profitable. In South Africa, an emerging trend among the youth is claims that a lot of money is being made through forex trading. With forex, I was told that predictions are based on market analysis so this excited me and gave me hope. The predictions are informed because there are various ways to determine the direction of the market. I attended a trading class where I learned how to trade. But I quickly realised that my passion, once again, was non-existent despite the fact that I was learning a lot. Most people make it seem as if anyone can do it, but this is not the case. A truth I discovered painfully, after losing a lot of money, is that if you have no passion for something like trading, the chances of making money are very little. In addition, trading is not passive income. It's a 24/7 business that requires your full attention.

If you are not passionate about something, don't pursue it because your achievements will be nothing more than mediocre.

Furthermore, forex trading is full of deceptive people who pretend to be making money in one way in order to lure other people into trading so they can make money off them. I met a few people who had lost other investors' money with devastating consequences. I quickly decided to leave forex behind.

Looking back on these disastrous moments of my crazy phase, I drew four key lessons explored in depth below:

1. Passion: If you are not passionate about something, don't pursue it because your achievements will be nothing more than mediocre. It won't bring you any joy, just frustration. These kinds of markets rely on losing and winning; someone has to

lose in order for someone else to win, and I was losing because I did not have the passion.

2. I was trying to study and learn to make money quickly; one of my favourite Bible verses reads: 'And every man that striveth for mastery is temperate in all things.' – 1 Corinthians 9:25. Which in my case means that if I wanted to achieve the success I desired, I needed to show some restraint and cautious discipline. This was hurting because I was hasty, and I was not taking time to learn the basics, as I later did with Bitcoin. I quickly learned that when you are passionate about something, mistakes actually drive you to learn. Yet the opposite happens when you are not passionate and have no interest other than making money.

3. Learning from your mistakes is pivotal when it comes to business because passion matures; passion often begins as an interest where you learn as you grow within it. Your interest is built upon passion. For instance, when you gain an interest in something for the first time, you are often jittery and nervous when you speak of this new-found interest, but with time you gain the language and expertise to confidently speak and learn about it. It is no longer just an interest, it becomes a lifestyle. Most importantly, passion breeds confidence in what you are doing, therefore it becomes easier to learn and gain valuable knowledge with time.

4. Lastly, at the end of this you may ask: is there such a thing as 'easy' money? My experiments had yielded such stressful results. My belief is that it *is* possible to make easy money, but it requires passion and dedication. The truth is, there are some who lose money trading, yet there are others who do make a profit. For me, Bitcoin was a form of easy money, especially for those like myself who got into it just as it was beginning. Bitcoin presented me with a clear opportunity and I realised the volatility and potential to make money. I wanted to run a profitable business, and Bitcoin presented me with

this opportunity. That is why I feel that your passion and your desired lifestyle should be aligned.

Once I had mapped out what I wanted my future to look like in terms of investment, I had a sense that I wanted to go into franchising. I chose a low-risk business which was Fish 'n Chips. The main reason why I chose this particular brand is because it's owned by a strong company that knows how to take care of its franchisees. Secondly, the business model is already established. Lastly, just because someone is selling, it does not mean that the business has failed; people sell for different reasons. Of course, this was a completely new territory for me so I made a few mistakes.

It is human nature to be compassionate and care about job security for people who have been working at a place for a long time. When I took over the franchise, I found myself having to play the catch-up game with employees, who knew things which I didn't know, as a first-time owner in the business and the area. It became harder to implement new strategies because they would either brush them off or tell me that they were tried before and never worked. I had no evidence of whether this was true or not. Soon enough, I noticed that the staff was creatively stealing from me and it took me a while to figure out how they were doing it. That is the downside of entering the business world so young. People want to undermine and abuse you. They cannot believe that a person who is young and fresh from university can be trusted with the power required to run a big business and even more so, run an already-established franchise.

A fish and chips store generally sells fish, sausages, chips and cool drinks. Our particular shop was sitting at a profit margin of 54 % for each sale on fish and chips, but not cool drinks in particular because the prices were regulated. Potatoes tend to fluctuate depending on the pricing farmers set, due to droughts and other factors. Within the business, I discovered the theft of potatoes was relatively easy because potatoes are purchased in kilograms, and you don't really know how many are in the bags. So you can't determine how many boxes of chips one bag of potatoes should make. The potatoes were being stolen, but it was impossible to steal the other products because we knew exactly how many pieces of fish and Russian sausages there were. The last straw for me was when an estimate of R7000 was stolen from the store; this seemed like an inside job. The continuous theft left a sour taste in my mouth so I decided to lease the store out to someone else, who faced similar issues within three months. I finally decided to change the staff and become more hands-on in managing the business. Finally, I involved the franchisor as I was not the first person with a store facing similar issues. The great thing about new staff is that I could groom them and grow a trusting relationship; the business was finally in a profitable position.

When venturing into a new business, market research is very important.

I learned six important lessons in running a franchise explored in depth below:

1. Find individuals who are willing to learn. Establish a trusting relationship and groom them in exactly how you want things to be done. Mentor them by giving them goals to achieve, and ensure that they are challenged on a daily basis to improve their morale. This way, as the owner, you are less 'hands-on' and the operational manager is able to take ownership of the store and how it makes a profit. I have also created a system of giving the manager an incentive for delivering peak performance.

2. I also monitor the store using digital surveillance which I can analyse remotely and if I pick up on an issue I can swiftly

address it with the manager. This also means that I am in direct liaison with one person whom I hold accountable for everything in the store.

3. I am constantly joining the networks relevant to my franchise business, where we exchange advice and share insights on how to run a successful franchise. Joining such networks helps you to gain the right advice to assist you when you are making big mistakes, and at times you are able to pre-empt a situation by learning from your peers.

4. In terms of a lease negotiation, you need to be pre-emptive of issues such as increases in rates, electricity, salaries, etc. Always attempt to keep your annual increase as low as possible.

5. Lastly, try not to run to the popular franchises. Initially my first choice was McDonalds because of its high success rate. It is quickly funded, but I found out that there's a 30-year waiting list. So you need to select a franchise that is managed by a well-established company and is highly likely to succeed without a long waiting period.

6. I now believe that franchising is not so crazy, and is the ideal business avenue for me. I often meet people who want to run a franchise, and my advice is simple. Firstly, find a well-established franchisor, and secondly get a good team behind you. A strong mother company is key in the success of your franchise. Often, franchises do not last because the franchisor is not available to offer hands-on help and advice.

After operating my fish and chips franchise for such an extended period, I decided that it was time to start my own franchise, Dag's Braai Corner. I thought of the food I loved the most growing up, and felt that I would start a franchise specialising in barbecued meat. I started off by creating the graphics for the business, found a location that seemed ideal, near the Midrand taxi rank, and created a website. The business opened and I felt that I was going to make money. After the business had been running for a short while, I realised that I had a problem. People were not buying food at our shop. I quickly evaluated the situation, and it became evident that the exact same food was being sold on the other side of the road at a cheaper price. The community of taxi drivers and commuters were already used to the hawkers, and they had a relationship.

When venturing into a new business, market research is very important and, at times, we overlook independent trading, which is very active in the market and economy. Competing against informal traders is nearly impossible because a restaurant model runs on large overheads, whereas they basically have very little to no overhead costs. As a result, the concept of Dag's Braai Corner in Midrand failed.

That was the last episode in my 'crazy' phase, the subject of Chapter Eight. I hurled myself into things which seemed like good ideas at the time, such as sports betting or binary trading. And I escaped as soon as I had learned my lesson. This is a phase that many entrepreneurs go through, and although a lot of money and resources can be wasted, I am grateful for this phase because it has given me the opportunity to present my mistakes in the hope that aspiring entrepreneurs will avoid the same pitfalls, save time and focus on their passion.

In business, entrepreneurs make mistakes and these mistakes are important. I believe in a principle of failing fast. Failing fast gives an entrepreneur the chance to learn pivotal lessons as quickly as possible. It is no lie that I lost a lot of money during this phase because there were times when I simply went overboard, and this made me realise that no amount of money can make up for passion.

For me, personally, my biggest strength is also my weakness. I am very inquisitive, as most entrepreneurs are. If someone said that they were making money one way or the other, I wanted in on that, without realising that most things are easier said than done. First of all, our paths are different and there are people who lie in order to make people fall for scams. Secondly, losing money to scammers is unnecessary. You need to take time to analyse claims made by people and research their companies and who they are. Lastly, failure is an important lesson on the road to success; the faster you engage with a new idea, the greater your chances of learning.

CHAPTER SEVEN: KEY LESSONS

1. Be crazy by all means, but don't risk a loss you cannot afford. I was quick to get into some crazy ideas such as sports betting, but got out just as quickly when I realised they didn't suit me. Or, in the case of Dag's Braai Corner, when I realised that the business model was unsustainable.

2. If a new investment such as a franchise tempts you, talk to people who are in it already. Ask them about the advantages and drawbacks; think long and hard before you take the plunge, as I did before my first fast-food venture.

3. Sound information is the basis of a viable business. My first franchise was difficult to operate because the staff didn't keep me well-informed. When I started from scratch again, it was with full control and reliable business figures, in the style of my grandfather.

4. A passive income is founded on years of hard work, and a passion for what you're doing. You're setting yourself up for disappointment if you start something not because it's a challenge, but purely because you want to make money. That's why I got out of forex trading.

5. A well-chosen franchise can be the start of something big. Efficiently managed to provide a service in popular demand, it can supply a steady income and opportunities for expansion. If this is your passion, success is highly likely. Just don't expect overnight riches.

Part Two

EIGHT

The history of money

This book is largely about cryptocurrency, the money of the future. And although money seems a commonplace thing which we handle every day, it is actually a complex phenomenon. And we will never understand the money of the future without learning how money came about in the first place. So, let's take a close look at the history of money, as a foundation for our later steps into the future. And we're going to start before there was any money at all.

There was the barter system: swapping something you could spare for something you needed. This was a convenient peer-to-peer system, with no middlemen to take their cut. It was an ideal system for the Stone Age. Let's imagine that we have a magic time-travel TV screen. When we punch in a date on the remote, it can bring us scenes from any year in history. And the year 70 000 BC brings up a movie of cavemen, sitting on the ground outside their rock shelter, shaping flint into sharp spearheads. As the pile of spearheads builds up, the cave family's stomachs are grumbling. It looks as if they'll sleep with empty stomachs, because there are no game animals in their valley.

But then their mouths start to water, for a hunter from the next valley walks up to their cave. And he's holding a juicy leg of mutton from a wild sheep that he speared at dawn in his own valley. But now his spear is blunt, and he needs a new point. He's been so busy hunting that he never learned how to shape flint – and in any case, there's no flint to be found in his area. On our magic screen, we see the deal go down: a dozen sharp spearheads in exchange for a tasty piece of meat. That's how barter works – fair exchange is no robbery.

We will never understand the money of the future without learning how money came about in the first place.

Punch in the year 3000 BC, and the scene changes to a dusty footpath where a farmer is driving a cow toward the gate of an ancient walled city in Mesopotamia. He enters the city's narrow, crowded streets and seeks out a merchant who might take the cow in exchange for things the farmer needs – including linen for his wife's new dress. After an argument and much waving of hands, the linen merchant sends the farmer to a butcher, who buys the cow off him for a handful of pretty shells. The farmer takes them on trust and goes back to the linen merchant. He gets his fabric for some shells and has plenty left over. He takes them back to his homestead and buries them under the mud floor for safekeeping. Everyone concerned is happy, because there is no need to handle large awkward objects such as livestock or sacks of grain. The middleman is now standing between buyer and seller, but this is not based on true money. When Joseph advised the Pharaoh of Egypt to prepare for lean years to come, it was grain that piled up in the royal stores, not coins. In those days, gold was scarce, but used mostly for jewellery. Archaeologists have unearthed clay tablets from 3000 BC which were the first ledgers: records of transactions involving barter items, taxes paid in grain by the king's subjects and wages paid to royal servants. Those records on the clay tablets were the first examples of what is called money of account: numbers written down in a ledger. The king sent out tax gatherers to strip the farmers of their harvests, because he needed grain to pay his courtiers and soldiers. For coins had yet to be invented.

The 'shekel' mentioned in the Bible was originally a sack of barley, and the name 'shekel' was only given to a coin much later. But such money of exchange had yet to appear in Mesopotamia. Let's punch in a few dates in search of the first real coin. And there it is, shining brightly at us from the screen in the year 600 BC. It weighs nearly five grams, an alloy of gold and silver, which was minted by King Alyattes of Lydia, a kingdom in the classical Greek world. Stamped on the coin is a roaring lion's head. At the marketplace in the Lydian city of Sardis, we follow a housewife who hands over the coin in exchange for one sheep. Then she pays a similar amount for three jars of wine. Maybe she's organising a wedding reception. Coinage appeared through necessity, as cultures and economies grew more complex. To expand, they needed a legal, widely-used store of value that was also a medium of exchange, and a unit that could be used to work out profit and loss. Something that could be carried in bulk, and used to pay for goods and services, or settle debts. Metal coins were durable and could be stamped with the image of the ruler who had issued them, like Alyattes. The age of metal coins had begun in the turbulent history of money.

Now we switch our magic screen to the early years in the history of metal coins. We are in the fifth century BC, at a bustling market in the city state of Athens, dominated by the classic temples on the rocky Acropolis. Silver coins are sparkling everywhere as the deals go down between people of this democracy, ruled by free citizens. The city states of Greece enjoy a booming economy, pushed upward by the discovery of a rich silver mine on Athenian territory and the introduction of Athenian silver coins. This new medium of exchange greases the economic wheels of the classical Greek world. The silver coins are widely accepted, and other regimes are soon stamping their own coinage. When the silver mines of Greece are exhausted, Athenian ships sail to Tartessos in south western Spain to bring back cargoes of precious metal.

Next, we pick up the magic remote and key in a scene from AD 1120 in China, ruled by the Song Dynasty, where billions of copper coins are in circulation. A wagon is bogged down in mud, and the driver whips his oxen in vain. As the camera zooms in on the stuck wagon's contents, we realise that it's laden with heavy sacks of copper coins. They are circular, with a hole in the middle, and can be strung like a necklace. To keep the cash flowing, Emperor Gaozong experimented with paper money, so that vast riches could be transported easily. And paper money supplemented coins for the next few centuries. Our TV time screen shows us several Chinese factories busy printing paper money, but they did not make enough to cause inflation.

Let's click on 1250, and switch from East to West, picturing a prosperous Swiss merchant clad in warm furs. He is weighing gold coins in his hand-held scales. This is a sign that silver's long run was coming to an end, as gold became a popular basis for currencies. Gold was scarcer than silver, and these coins had a high value because of the short supply. By this stage, you could still feel your medium of exchange and store of value, but you could no longer smell or eat it.

Key in 1544, and there sits King Henry VIII of England. He's talking to his financial adviser in a room at Hampton Court Palace. 'I need a million for my war with France,' says Henry. 'But I can't tax the people any more. So how can I raise money?'

The wily adviser tells him, 'Mint as many coins as you need, Sire!'

'But I've only got so much silver,' says the fat king.

'That's no problem,' says the money man. 'All over Europe,

silver coins contain 12% copper. But you can mint a million containing 90% copper.'

'Brilliant!' says Henry. 'Who's to know?'

But just about everybody worked out what was going on, and in the end nobody would touch Henry's worthless inflated coinage – pennies disguised as pounds.

Now we go to 1600, and a royal counting house in Seville. Accountants are unpacking chests of gold items newly unloaded from galleons which have come from Peru and Mexico. The Spanish authorities used the Aztec and Inca riches from the Americas to flood Europe with gold coins – which lost value because they were no longer so scarce. Scarcity creates value. And when gold became more plentiful, value dropped.

In the mid 1700s, European nations introduced the gold standard, by which a paper banknote could be exchanged for a gold coin. Our imaginary TV screen shows us 1765 in London, with Bank of England account holders waiting in a queue to swop paper for precious metal. To this day, a 20 pound note issued by the Bank of England still bears the words: I promise to pay the bearer on demand. But nowadays, that's a big fat lie. If you made that demand, they'd give you another note just like it, or four five pound coins. The same pledge was once printed on South African currency, but these days the Reserve Bank is making no promises at all.

We are now living in an age where change is more rapid, more unpredictable than ever before.

In the 20th century, countries such as France, the UK and the US came off the gold standard. Their currencies rose or fell in value depending on circumstances. The US still has an enormous amount of gold stashed underground in Fort Knox, but the precious metal is not there to back up the US dollar. No – because we are in an era where the currencies of the world are based on trust. They are known as 'fiat' currencies, from a Latin expression meaning roughly: 'Let it be'. A R20 note is actually a worthless piece of paper, but it's accepted gladly all over South Africa, and will buy you a hot drink in any cafe. Because people believe in it, trust it, and use it as a medium of exchange and a store of value. A rand is reliable as a note, a coin, or a number in a bank's online ledger.

But with fiat paper currencies came the danger that some cash-strapped governments would rashly print more paper money than their economies are worth. In such cases, disaster always follows. It happened in Weimar Germany after World War I and in Brazil during the 1960s. Fortunes vanished into thin air as those currencies crashed. Punch in a date in the not too distant past. And the magic TV will show me, Mpho Dagada, listening to the sad tale of a Zimbabwean who sold her house in Bulawayo and emigrated to Joburg, to get away from Mugabe's enforcers. She tells me how the proceeds of the house sale went into a blocked bank account which she wasn't allowed to touch. Then Robert Gabriel Mugabe needed money to pay his debts, and like Henry VIII, he inflated the Zim dollar.

Bob didn't need to mess around with copper and silver – he simply revved up the government printing press and produced astronomic numbers of banknotes, with a face value which was well in excess of the whole country's worth. Soon the Mugabe regime was on a hyperinflation treadmill, printing trillion dollar notes which would buy only half a dozen eggs. Fortunes were destroyed. In the end, the Zimbabwean economy went over to using the Rand and the US dollar, to stop the inflation.

Investors can no longer taste, eat, smell or fondle their currency, now in the form of fragile paper. But fiat currencies are reaching the end of their usefulness. Something that dates back to the mid-1700s is well past its sell-by date in the online age of today. The world is always evolving, and the old ways linger on as obstacles to progress. Across the centuries, this has always been the case. But Humankind has always got smart and found new solutions to keep the wheels of the economy turning. In early centuries, inventors met the challenges of a rapidly changing world with such brilliant ideas as coinage, the gold standard and paper currency. But the online world is leaving these worn-out concepts behind in the 21st century.

We are now living in an age where change is more rapid, more unpredictable than ever before. And as usual, someone – Satoshi Nakamoto – got smart and found a solution to the outmoded paper money that is holding the world economy back. A revolution in currency is already under way, as money launches into cyberspace, along with many other elements of our daily life. We are living in the early years of the Cryptocurrency Age.

CHAPTER EIGHT: KEY LESSONS

1. Peer-to-peer barter was the first economic trans-action, back in the Stone Age. A surplus was exchanged for a needed commodity.

2. Tokens such as shells met the needs of the early civilisations. They were convenient to carry, and found great use in small urban societies.

3. Silver coins fuelled the expansion of classical states and greased the wheels of their economies. This was an advance on tokens, because scarce silver also acted as a store of value as well as a medium of exchange. Chinese emperors issued copper cash for small purchases and printed paper money worth much more.

4. Gold was very scarce, so it dominated silver coinage in Europe. Then gold was used to back paper banknotes. Nowadays the paper currencies we use are not backed by precious metal. We use paper fiat (let it be) currencies based on trust. But when this trust breaks down in hyperinflation, other exchange media take over – even such items as cigarettes.

5. Blockchain and Bitcoin are now pioneering a new online financial world. Cryptocurrencies will replace fiat money in the end, as they are faster, better and more convenient than all the earlier forms of currency.

NINE

Bitcoin

T hen came the great turning point in my life, and I was led up to it by my curiosity. I had noted that money was moved around in most of these get-rich-quick schemes using cryptocurrency. Bitcoin in particular was used to pay Kipi membership fees and investments. So I began to research Bitcoin, little suspecting that it would make me a wealthy man in a short time.

Bitcoin is a digital currency in which encryption techniques are used to regulate the generation of units of currency and verify the transfer of funds, operating independently of a central bank. The origin of Bitcoin is in the digital space, which often further confuses people because it seems as if this currency came out of nowhere. A central figure in the origin of Bitcoin is Satoshi Nakamoto, an anonymous individual – or possibly a group of people – who created the original concept.

In the international markets, Bitcoin has always roused debate and contention; it did very well in the markets at its inception. It was not the first digital currency, but it was the first to be decentralised – everywhere and nowhere at the same time. Bitcoin is not owned by a single entity like Facebook or Microsoft. You cannot point to a building or a server it operates from.

As a digital currency, it is used across the world to pay for goods and services, as well as Ponzi scheme joining fees. It follows the ideas set out on white paper by the mysterious Satoshi Nakamoto, whose true identity has yet to be confirmed. Bitcoin offers the promise of lower transaction fees than traditional online payment mechanisms and it is operated by a decentralised authority, unlike government-issued currencies. It finally made sense to me why Kipi had chosen to use this untraceable mode of payment. In addition, many schemes I came across required Bitcoin as a mode of transferring money because it was an anonymous payment system that isn't regulated by a government or bank. People in these schemes looked for Bitcoin high and low.

Remember my Kipi experience? It was there that I first heard about Bitcoin, and it was in helping my fellow investors that I went online and found a website called localBitcoins.com where I engaged with different sellers in the local market.

Bitcoin is a digital currency in which encryption techniques are used to regulate the generation of units of currency and verify the transfer of funds, operating independently of a central bank.

On the website, you simply register an account using your email address, and then you see a list of sellers willing to trade their Bitcoin at various prices. I noticed that their pricing differed slightly and when I enquired about this, I was informed that market supply and demand determined the price. Bitcoin and other cryptocurrencies operate within a market similarly to mainstream currencies and commodities. The only difference is that the value isn't determined by a government, political climates or how much money was printed; instead the value is based on demand and availability of the coin.

I made an offer to one of the sellers on localBitcoins.com, and they accepted my offer. After my bad experiences with these systems, I still felt slightly paranoid when the process was explained to me; all the money had to be paid up front, and this reminded me of the money I had previously lost in Ponzi schemes. They assured me that I would receive the Bitcoins because they were kept in an escrow account on localBitcoins.com until the funds reflected in the seller's account.

The Bitcoin was released to me in a Bitcoin wallet – a digital platform where Bitcoin is stored. Within a matter of a single day, the value of the Bitcoin spiked from US$200 to US$1242. This meant that we would make well over ZAR 10 000 if we were to resell the coin at its current rate.

I sold the virtual coin, and split the money with my fellow investor. At the time, US$1 was equal to 13 South African Rands. When I received a phone call the next day, asking 'Can you do what you did again?' I explained that I did nothing to manipulate the price and the returns, because the Bitcoin did that all by itself. Bitcoin had achieved what no currency had ever achieved: its value increased overnight by over 500%, and I was sold. I wanted to know more about cryptocurrency, its origins and what made it so volatile. Despite knowing a lot about money and growing up in a family that often spoke about money, I was still in awe of what had happened and, with enthusiasm, I jumped straight in.

As I navigated the Bitcoin market, I found ways to directly purchase the coin and sell it again at a higher price (demand and supply). It was exciting for me because I believed that this was a legitimate way to create a relatively passive income for myself. At the time I was not sure what people used Bitcoin for, but it was an effective store of value. This was interesting because of Bitcoin's volatile nature. And I decided to use the platform where

I had bought my first Bitcoin, to trade in the cryptocurrency. Back in 2013, Bitcoin had not taken off, and its validity as a currency was under scrutiny. For some, it was a currency, while others claimed it was a commodity. To this day, it remains a subject of much debate in the international financial markets. After a few months of trading, I decided to buy more Bitcoin because I noticed that Bitcoin's fluctuation was steadily increasing – and despite the fluctuation, its value was increasing by the day. People began to use the term 'cryptocurrency'. The transparency of this new currency ensured that governments could not regulate it or dictate its direction. I needed this kind of assurance. I needed to know that my money would not be determined by a third party whose greed could affect my returns.

Many prominent businessmen and millionaires across the world believed in the power of this new currency because its value was determined by the market – the people. I discovered a fascinating aspect that contributed to the rapid growth of Bitcoin – it wasn't printed money, and its value wasn't determined by quantity. In Africa where many economies are controlled by 'big men', hyperinflation can run rampant – Zimbabwe being a prime example. In the light of this eventuality, cryptocurrency has been referred to as a solution in need of a problem.

At university, I was making big plans that could change my life, for better or for worse. As I grew from novice to expert in trading, storing and buying Bitcoin, I decided to employ someone to help me supply Bitcoin. Bitcoin is a 24-hour business that requires you to be available at all times to supply the coin to people. I was still a student, and it was challenging because I had to attend to my varsity schedule and keep my newly founded business operational. Again, I also had to do well at school so that my family wasn't aware of what I was getting up to. I often felt it was a shame that something so amazing and interesting had to be kept secret.

The Bitcoin community generally operated at odd times and it was growing at a rapid pace. So I needed a partner in my trading business. I had to channel the work ethic of both my parents and grandfather. I had to commit to this new entity and make sure that it worked for me in order to reach my goals. I have been asked so many times by curious people, 'Mpho, how do I use this Bitcoin you speak about?' and my answer is always the same. The first way to get started with Bitcoin, and the first way to get started with anything, is by actually purchasing it and owning it. You then have to register with an exchange which usually takes the form of a website. There are a number of exchanges available on the Bitcoin.org website. You don't have to own and purchase a Bitcoin to register and create a Bitcoin account. Usually you just sign up for a user account by providing basic information and then you receive an email that requires you to activate your account. Then the registration process starts.

The beauty of Bitcoin is that it works with the masses. The more people join and invest, the more valuable the cryptocurrency becomes, and they all contribute to its growing value.

There is a Know-Your-Customer verification procedure that needs to be completed in order to properly use a Bitcoin exchange. This is a procedure that is designed to store your personal information. It also brings in a sense of credibility because it makes you a part of the exchange. I remember that many Ponzi schemes did not require much in the form of personal details, they just wanted money – quick money! You need to confirm your phone number as most exchanges send a code to that number as a text message. You then have to provide a personal ID, such as your ID document, driver's licence, birth certificate or passport.

People who question Bitcoin are concerned that they will lose money in a system that makes the same promises as a Ponzi scheme. Even with the intense media coverage on Bitcoin, some accounts are a little sketchy. There has been a flood of articles and testimonials by people who communicated both their success and failure with Bitcoin.

My book comes from the perspective of someone who has seen success with Bitcoin. And in these pages I will give an in-depth explanation of everything that you need to know to adopt Bitcoin as a customary currency. It is a lengthy explanation and a necessary one. But there is a beautiful history tied in with this amazing technology, and I hope my accounts of it will inspire you to join the cryptocurrency revolution.

Firstly, the most fascinating thing about Bitcoin is its origin and the concepts behind it. One cannot speak about Bitcoin without paying homage to the man behind it. Satoshi Nakamoto is said to be a developer who saw the way our old familiar payment systems operated. His aim was not to derail them but to improve them. His idea originated during the financial crisis of 2008. Many people were affected by it, and they needed some mechanism to save their money. Governments were printing extra money in an attempt to meet the financial demands prevalent at the time. This resulted in the devaluation of the currency. Bank involvement was proving to be a disadvantage, and that is when Satoshi stepped in with Bitcoin – a financial system that was independent of any government. And most importantly, a system that did not need a bank as the middleman for all transactions. Since then, Bitcoin has become more than just a form of payment. It is now a means of investing your money in a trustworthy system that is well-nigh impossible to scam.

The beauty of Bitcoin is that it works with the masses. The more people join and invest, the more valuable the cryptocurrency becomes, and they all contribute to its growing value. The users determine the Bitcoin price through supply and demand. The amount of Bitcoins that will be produced is limited to 21 million – a target that is set to be reached by 2140.

The limit to Bitcoin is the major reason why people should join now and reap all the early benefits. It is also advisable for businesses to start using Bitcoin as a form of payment because it has a number of advantages. For starters, the very low fees in relation to other forms of transaction are a bonus. Bitcoin payments can be converted into the currency of your choice, which makes them convenient in many countries. Bitcoin is global. Every country views it and uses it in the same way. For consumers the same is true. They don't have to use physical cash as a means of payment and don't have to wait for a bank to go through its procedure. You can transact and make payments at any time, even on weekends and holidays, without being confined to business hours. An online payment is processed immediately.

Bitcoin operates using the so-called Open Ledger. Everyone and anyone can see each financial transaction that happens on the network in real time, from any part of the world. This gives confidence to potential investors because they can see the transactions taking place. And they can see the growth.

Many people worry about the anonymity of Bitcoin and whether or not their full identity is disclosed in the system. The answer is simple. Your anonymity is subject to a wallet address and the open public ledger known as a blockchain, which tracks any incoming and outgoing transfers to and from any address at any given time. Once someone knows your wallet address, they can monitor it at the www.blockchain.info website. Here, they'll see your current transactions and also every other transaction tied to your Bitcoin address. But there are extensive ways of ensuring anonymity – employed mostly by people with something to hide, such as illegal deals or attempts to cheat the taxman. But using external sources to keep your anonymity can be very risky, and it also brings the middleman back into the game. One way to ensure anonymity is by generating a new wallet address every time you make a transaction, so that it's not tied to any other transactions you've made in the past. Another way is to keep your wallet address a secret.

Like every other new technology, there is a difficulty in learning to trust it and working out its differences to existing technologies. It is human nature to cling to current norms, and accepting Bitcoin technology can be difficult at first. When explaining Bitcoin, I compare it to the introduction of the internet. When the internet was first introduced, people never thought that it would ever become the essential tool it is today. The vast majority took baby steps into the reality that it was here to stay. They were so comfortable in their tried and tested ways that they dismissed the internet. They thought it was temporary. Like the internet, Bitcoin is here to disrupt the future and take over – in the best way, of course. Many people have already jumped in, and this is a positive step.

It is always advisable to do your research. You also need to figure out exchange rates. Experts give the following three tips when checking out the best exchange rates:

1. Whenever you want to exchange Bitcoin for physical currency, or vice versa, make sure to check the current Bitcoin price before you do anything else. Over the past few years, Bitcoin exchanges have started offering a 'fixed' price per Bitcoin, assuming that you successfully complete the transaction within a certain time frame. For example, when converting BTC (Bitcoin) into local currency, a user must complete the transfer within 60 seconds in order to get the current price. Failure to do so may result in a different price at the time of transaction, which can either be higher or lower.

2. Keep a close eye on the Bitcoin exchange rate for your local currency at all times to maximise your profits and reduce your losses. Some good sources of data are websites such as Bitcoinwisdom.com, Cryptotrader.com and Coinmarketcap.com.

3. Keep in mind that there will usually be an exchange fee at some point during the transaction, so be sure to understand how

much that will be. Some Bitcoin exchange platforms take a small cut when your buy and sell order has been executed, whereas others will simply charge you more or pay you less overall. Plus, additional fees may be applicable when withdrawing your physical currency to a bank account.

There are two types of Bitcoin exchanges: peer-to-peer and regular. A regular exchange is one where an order book is used to match buy and sell orders from people. Neither the buyer nor the seller know who the other person is, and this goes back to the level of anonymity that Bitcoin allows. But Bitcoin was first created to allow peer-to-peer transactions. This means that you have a one-on-one relationship with the person you are transacting with – because you have access to most of their details. This in most cases will form a relationship of trust with another investor. And in a way, someone will be liable for the money, should Bitcoin disappear. When it comes to security, Bitcoin generates a lot of discussion. This is because the same aspects that give Bitcoin its level of freedom also create a security concern for people, and this is a fair point as there are security risks associated with any financial vehicle – including Bitcoin.

To understand the topic of liability, I recommend Prypto's explanation of this grey area, which follows. Bitcoin is an unregulated and ungoverned digital currency. Which means that any associated services are equally unregulated and ungoverned. However, in certain parts of the world, there are some regulations you will have to obey. It remains unclear who will be liable if a Bitcoin exchange is hacked – or if the service shuts down without a warning. Most of the bigger, more reputable exchanges have systems in place to protect clients from financial risk – but only up to a certain limit. If the exchange is hacked, or your funds are lost in any way while stored on its platform, the exchange will reimburse you out of its own pocket. This helps to put sceptical consumers' minds at ease because it gives them a sense of assurance that their money will not disappear.

Some economists would even go as far as saying that a Bitcoin exchange is a self-regulating platform such as NASDAQ. However, as big as NASDAQ is, it claims immunity from computer crashes. Which means this exchange won't reimburse any funds lost in a computer crash. Bitcoin exchanges operate in a different manner. The amount of protection that exchanges may offer to customers may well depend on two things: where they are registered; and the licensing requirements (or lack thereof) of that jurisdiction. Storing your Bitcoins on an exchange for more than a day or two is never a good idea. Because if that exchange were to cease operating for any reason at all, your options would be determined by the local laws of the place where the exchange is registered. Generally speaking, the tougher the licensing requirements, the more protection you are likely to be offered. But you should check the terms and conditions of any exchange you use and the level of protection that it may – or may not – offer you.

More and more Bitcoin exchanges have opened the door to receiving independent third-party audits. An auditor can verify whether a Bitcoin exchange is solvent enough to continue its operations. The auditor can get the security measures stress-tested to see if the user data is protected properly. Security is a very important aspect of the Bitcoin world. Without digital security in place, your digital wealth could get stolen at any time. Bitcoin developers have been aware of this problem from the beginning and have enabled a feature inside the Bitcoin client that lets you encrypt your 'wallet' with a difficult-to-crack password.

Chapter Nine gets down to the main subject of this book. I tell the story of my discovery of cryptocurrencies and how I took my first steps with Bitcoin. Like everything else, Bitcoin has its pros and cons. As someone who has seen success with it, I vouch that there are more pros than cons. There is a reason why I have been supporting this platform for so long, and God has allowed me the opportunity to speak of it with pride.

Despite my young years, I am a self-made wealthy man. The financial freedom I have gained enables me to achieve much in life – and most importantly it has given me the wherewithal to invest in multiple businesses. I learned lessons which I would like to pass on to other members of my generation. I see us as the generation which will put all things on the map for those to come. We who live in in a digital age are very tech-savvy. It will take some time, but I believe that we will understand how fortunate we are to be exposed to the innovations of the present day. Bitcoin is one of these innovations and it will be around for a long time.

The biggest concern with joining any financial scheme is the question of how secure it is – and how it could benefit or ruin your life. Every time I heard of a scheme, I would do some research so that I had enough knowledge to join it. I would look at minor details to make sure that I would benefit instead of lose money. Of course, I had my fair share of failures, and when I look back, there were many red flags I didn't notice. But I would have been alerted to the dangers if I'd taken a little more time before I dived in. That's why I host online classes and live seminars to teach people about cryptocurrency. The aim of my investment in the future currency initiative is to create financial freedom for ordinary people who just want to make their lives better for themselves and for their families. I do this by offering affordable courses on cryptocurrencies like Bitcoin, which I believe will shape the future of an intelligent economic society.

I show clients how to invest their funds at a very practical, personal level. My course is basically a step-by-step guide which will teach clients how to invest in cryptocurrencies and how to maintain a healthy digital currency investment portfolio. I have never advised people to just dive right in without making an informed decision. And my responsibility is to ensure that clients get the full positive experience from using Bitcoin.

The biggest advantage presented by Bitcoin's underlying blockchain technology is a completely transparent trading system. On top of that, Bitcoin transactions invoke very low or non-existent fees. But the general public needs to learn about this amazing technology. Many people are suspicious, sceptical and wary of financial innovations – especially those who have fallen victim to scams. The prospect of meeting up with strangers for peer-to-peer transactions is also a risk in itself. Luckily, there are local cryptocurrency groups all around the world. These are a great way to get to know people with a passion for cryptocurrency, and there are no membership fees.

Prypto has listed 10 great ways to use Bitcoin, and I will expand on these later on in the book.

1. As an investment vehicle.
2. As an educational tool.
3. For everyday needs.
4. For buying luxuries.
5. For donations to charities.
6. For online games.
7. For investing in precious metals.
8. As a gift.
9. To pay bills.
10. As a social experiment.

Cryptocurrencies trade in a volatile market, with exchange rates that can fluctuate wildly over a single day, or in an hour. Bitcoin is the best known and most valuable cryptocurrency, but there are many others to explore, including Litecoin, Monero and Ripple. When you buy or receive cryptocurrency, you are given a digital key to the address of that currency. You can use this key to access and validate or approve transactions. You need a place to keep your key safe – and that's your cryptocurrency wallet.

A Bitcoin wallet is the place where you store all the information about your transactions. This wallet stores your funds just like a bank account. It allows you to send and receive funds. It's no exaggeration to say that a Bitcoin wallet is the single most important thing to protect. As soon as you have the Bitcoin wallet software installed on your computer or mobile device, you will be presented with a Bitcoin wallet address. This is the identification number by which you are known as a member of the Bitcoin network. It acts as your account number to send, receive, and store Bitcoins.

But there's more to a Bitcoin wallet than just the address. It also contains the public and private key for each of your Bitcoin addresses. Your private key is a randomly generated string of numbers and letters which allows you to spend Bitcoins. A private key is always mathematically related to the Bitcoin wallet address, but is impossible to reverse engineer thanks to a strong encryption code base.

You have a variety of wallets to choose from:

Desktop wallets. Software like Cryptonator allows you to send and store cryptocurrency addresses and also connects to the network to track transactions.

Online wallets. Cryptocurrency keys are stored online by exchange platforms like Coinbase or Circle and can be accessed from anywhere.

Mobile wallets. Apps like Blockchain Store encrypt your Bitcoin keys so that you can make payments using your mobile device.

Paper wallets. Some websites offer paper wallet services, generating a piece of paper with two QR codes on it. One code is the public address at which you receive cryptocurrency, and the other is your private address that you can use for spending.

Hardware wallets. You can use a USB device created specifically to store Bitcoin electronically along with your private address keys.

Cryptocurrencies are known for being secure and providing a level of anonymity. Transactions in them cannot be faked or reversed and they tend to have low fees, making them more reliable and affordable than conventional currency. Their decentralised nature means that they are available to everyone, unlike banks which can be choosy when it comes to clients. Cryptocurrency markets have been known to take off explosively, transforming a small investment into a large sum overnight. But the value can also drop like a stone, even faster than it rose! People who look to invest in cryptocurrencies should be aware of this market volatility and the risks they take when buying.

Because of the level of anonymity they offer, cryptocurrencies are often associated with illegal activity, particularly on the dark web. Users should be careful when choosing which cryptocurrency to buy. Always consult credible sources when trying to invest in cryptocurrency. Some websites are only there to scam people out of their money. And the only safe way to ensure that you get the most from the experience is to do the research.

Here's how to start Bitcoin trading: the simplest way to trade Bitcoin for a profit is, of course, person-to-person, and this simply means that you approach someone who is selling their Bitcoin. You will negotiate a price, pay the person and they will send you their address and public key digitally or physically. You can form a trust with this person and they can share some of their regular buyers with you – and vice-versa.

1. A Bitcoin can be traded for cash, gold and even cars. A popular website among people who trade is called localbitcoins.com where you deal with buyers and sellers one-on-one.

2. Another option is entering a Bitcoin Exchange which works as a virtual meeting place for people who want to buy and sell Bitcoins at an agreed market price. It works much like a stock exchange or a futures market. Price discovery drives these exchanges, so you will find out what the true market value is based on supply and demand.

Here's how you can make money in Bitcoin exchanges. An exchange provides a convenient platform to buy and sell cryptocurrencies; if you visit *https://Bitcoin.org/en/exchanges* you will find a comprehensive list of verified Bitcoin exchanges where you can sign up. Trading in Bitcoin is known for offering more trading opportunities than traditional forex currencies, and here are some ways in which you can make a reasonable profit.

1. Bitcoin is known for being a volatile currency so this provides a variation into how many trades you can make. Leverage ratios for traditional forex are also limited to 50:1 now, so Bitcoin offers traders substantial 'leverage' beyond that limit. It is calculated that Bitcoin gives you 6.8x to 18.6x the leverage of EUR and USD.

2. With Bitcoin, you can move between exchanges and use different currency pairs which are still fairly easy to find.

3. There have been reports that Bitcoin is basically uninfluenced by the fluctuation of mainstream currencies and commodities including EUR, USD, gold and interest rates.

4. Bitcoin pricing is directly influenced by demand, so the more people transact, the higher the price of the Bitcoin goes.

CHAPTER NINE: KEY LESSONS

1. Bitcoin is the biggest online encrypted currency. It is accepted worldwide as the future of currency in an online world and fulfils all the functions of a genuine currency. It is a scarce, secure medium of exchange and store of value as well as a unit of account.

2. Bitcoin price is very volatile, but the long-term overall trend is upward. The current volatility makes for an exciting trading environment, in these early days of the world's most desirable, yet largely misunderstood cryptocurrency.

3. It is regulated by a worldwide online system, not by any bank or government. This alarms some politicians and bankers, who feel threatened by the decentralised currency's ability to do without their costly services.

4. Cryptocurrencies are traded on a secure online open ledger called blockchain. This is open to anyone who cares to inspect it, and the record can never be erased. Blockchain makes cryptocurrencies possible, as well as many other future systems in every field of endeavour.

5. Cryptocurrencies, including Bitcoin, are the wave of the future. Like the internet, before it conquered the globe, they are unfamiliar and misunderstood by many. Despite some negative media coverage, Bitcoin is a currency just like the Rand, Pound or Dollar. It cannot be compared with scams such as Ponzi schemes, chain letters or pyramid schemes.

TEN

Is Bitcoin money?

When I first began to explore the world of cryptocurrencies, I heard people arguing, and some said Bitcoin wasn't money. After all, they said, you can't handle it; you could never toss a Bitcoin to call heads or tails at the start of a soccer match. These people sounded so sure of themselves that I thought of doing a bit of research to find out how the financial experts defined money. This led me into fascinating historical highways and byways. After my historical studies, I now had a foundation upon which I could build my investigation of what money is. When I looked in a good dictionary, I read: money is a current medium of exchange, and this medium of exchange includes coins and banknotes.

But to qualify as true money, I read that a currency has to do several jobs. First of all, money is meant to work as a medium of exchange that is more effective than the old peer-to-peer barter system. Secondly, money must be a unit of account, in order to determine the value of an item and measure profit and loss. Thirdly, money must be convenient, portable, durable and divisible into fractions for small purchases. And the fourth job is to stay scarce, to act as a desirable store of value for the investor. Not all currencies do the fourth job well, I realised, thinking back to the hyperinflation villains I had researched, from Henry the Eighth to Mugabe the First. Sadly, the value of money can shrink with inflation and rise with deflation. That rising value might sound good. But when a country such as Japan was hit by deflation, salaries were cut. And supermarket prices didn't drop until after the wages were reduced, so the cost of living went up. Deflation can cause suffering, just like inflation.

Bitcoin may be the best form of currency to emerge in the digital age. But as with anything new, it will take time for the world to fully adopt the digital currency.

I sat down and wrote the four properties of money on a piece of paper, then thought about Bitcoin and how well this cryptocurrency fulfilled them. As a scarce item, tick! As a durable store of value, tick! As a convenient, easily portable medium of exchange with denominations, tick! So I came to the conclusion that Bitcoin was indeed money, since it met all the criteria. Bitcoin has even exceeded the intended function of hard cash.

My research came to an end with the finding that yes – Bitcoin is money. And from then on, I had the facts at my disposal, which enabled me to win debates against people who claimed cryptocurrencies were no good for tossing heads or tails. I came to the conclusion that throughout world history, civilisations have created new forms of money. And although commodities like gold still offer a quality store of value, Bitcoin may be the best form of currency to emerge in the digital age. But as with anything new, it will take time for the world to fully adopt the digital currency.

I thought long and hard about pursuing a policy of investment, as well becoming active as a Bitcoin trader. But before I could go ahead, there was a mystery I had to solve. It was my grandfather who set me off on a new quest, during a visit to Venda. He asked, 'Where does this Bitcoin come from? I understand your explanation about how it could replace hard cash. But I'm still dubious, because it's not dug out of the earth, or harvested like mangos from a tree.'

I said that, while I'd heard of it, I wasn't sure what it meant. I assured him it was certainly worth looking into. And as I drove back to Jozi after the family visit, I resolved to become a fundi on Bitcoin mining, whatever that process turned out to be. I was well aware that the bright shiny golden Bitcoins I had seen in illustrations had never existed. And I was equally sure that no mining engineers had ever sunk a shaft to reach a rich vein of BTC far under the earth. With paper money a government decides when to print and distribute money. This is the so-called fiat currency. But Bitcoin doesn't have a central government. I spoke to experts and even had the opportunity to visit a 'mine' where BTC was extracted – from very powerful computers. Mining is an important and integral part of Bitcoin. It ensures fairness – while keeping the Bitcoin network stable, safe and secure. As my research proceeded, I filled a notebook with my findings. The word 'mining' is slightly misleading because it suggests that coins are dug out of the ground literally. Bitcoin mining is simply the process of adding more Bitcoins to the digital currency ecosystem. The Bitcoins have to be generated through a computational process called mining. This is done by letting powerful computer hardware calculate complex mathematical equations which can be done at any time of the day. This makes miners an important factor in the Bitcoin network. This system gives something that I had been craving from other financial schemes – the feeling of importance. Bitcoin allows me to control things from my end, and all my effort is proven with the rewards I get back. There are certain similarities to how other resources, like gold, are mined. Unlike the printing of crazy nonstop paper money in countries such as Zimbabwe, Bitcoin ensures that no more coins are generated than the originally intended amount. As I have mentioned before, there will only be 21 million Bitcoins in circulation by 2140. The Bitcoin mining process has seen an evolution. It went from being a disregarded project to being one of the most important processes of the Bitcoin world. Bitcoin miners use special software to solve problems in maths. These problems involve the processing, checking and validation of Bitcoin transactions all over the world. In return for the work, the guys who operate these very expensive computers are given the right – by the network itself, not any government – to issue a block of Bitcoins.

This is a clever way to issue the currency and also creates an incentive for more people to mine. And since the miners' computers are the ones that approve the Bitcoin deals, more miners mean a more secure network. The Bitcoin network automatically changes the difficulty of the maths problems, depending on how fast they are being solved. In the early days, Bitcoin miners took a long time to solve these maths problems with their computers. But soon they discovered that the powerful graphics cards used for gaming were much better suited to this kind of work. Graphics cards are faster, they use more electricity and generate a lot of heat. And they are very expensive.

The first commercial Bitcoin mining products included chips that were reprogrammed for mining Bitcoin; these chips were faster but still power hungry. ASIC, or Application Specific Integrated Circuit chips, were specially designed for Bitcoin mining. ASIC technology makes the process faster while using less power. As the popularity of Bitcoin increases, more miners join the network, which makes the maths problems more difficult for individuals to solve. To beat this, miners now work together in groups, and find solutions faster than individuals ever could, working alone. Each miner is rewarded according to the amount of work he or she gets done.

Bitcoin mining is simply the process of adding more Bitcoins to the digital currency ecosystem.

This chapter addresses the question many people ask: how can Bitcoin be money when it consists of bits and bytes somewhere in cyberspace? One might as well ask why a cafe is prepared to see value in a grubby paper R20 note, when it's offered in payment for a cup of coffee. Recorded in blockchain, Satoshis will long outlive paper fiat currency, and they are more reliable. Because they are locked into a decentralised control system which is immune to outside tampering. I have also recorded my investigations into the generation of BTC by the so-called miners.

The first property of money is scarcity, and there will only ever be 21 million Bitcoins in the world by 2140. No person can create extra Bitcoins to trigger inflation, as Robert Mugabe did with the Zimbabwe dollar. Secondly, money needs to be durable. For digital currency, this is an open and shut case, as it's not exposed to the external elements that cause damage. It cannot be shredded, melted down or torn up. With Bitcoin, transactions are traceable. When I asked about denominations, the Bitcoin exchange staff explained to me that each Bitcoin (or BTC) can be divided to eight decimal places. A Millibit is 0.001 BTC, a Bit is 0.000001 BTC and a Satoshi is 0.00000001 BTC. That's a millionth part of a Bitcoin, divided by 100. Even when BTC prices hit the financial stratosphere, a Satoshi will get you a cup of coffee. Thinking about portability, I ticked off all the places where I could store BTC and carry out transactions: a Bitcoin-specific hardware wallet, a tablet, computer, or even a smartphone. Enormous wealth can be securely stored in cyberspace, without having to build a Fort Knox, as the Americans did.

CHAPTER TEN: KEY LESSONS

1. Bitcoin is just as trustworthy as paper fiat currency, and performs all the same functions. It is actually more effective and convenient as a durable medium of exchange, accounting token and store of value.

2. Bitcoin is 'mined' by supercomputers in a worldwide network. By cross-checking and working out the validity of Bitcoin transactions which happen in their millions every hour, the miners win the right to issue a new block of BTC. This becomes more expensive and less profitable as the number increases.

3. Mining will stop when 21 million Bitcoins have been produced in 2140. This point is estimated, based on the rate at which BTC are created. When all of these coins are in circulation, Bitcoin will be a true world currency, acceptable in every country. There will be no reason for the wild swings in price caused by supply and demand that we experience in the current era.

4. Cryptocurrencies do not inflate, as paper money can. Based on a decentralised system, they cannot be used as playthings by unscrupulous bankers or desperate governments. And BTC has already played the role of a hedge against government-triggered inflation in countries such as Venezuela and Zimbabwe.

5. Bitcoin can be used to pay for small purchases, which adds to its all-round convenience. It is already in use to pay in restaurants, supermarkets and theatres. Even when BTC is a mature currency, the fractional Satoshi will be small enough for everyday transactions.

ELEVEN

Banking and blockchain

While it may seem strange initially to apply the term wallet to Bitcoin, a simple Bitcoin wallet is of prime importance. The wallet is software which lives on your computer or device. It stores and protects the BTC you possess and guarantees safe transactions with other BTC wallets. It's peer-to-peer, like those ancient barter deals, but without many of the hassles, costs and insecurities of dealing in fiat paper currencies. Ironically, I learned that the most secure wallet is one that's printed out on paper, backed up, and locked away in safe places.

The Bitcoin wallet is your personal interface where you buy and sell your Bitcoins. It is embodied in the form of an app, website or device. There are different storage systems you can use, for example, computer hardware or an app, to set up a 'hot wallet'. Computer hardware is available for people who have large amounts of Bitcoin and need maximum security.

Computer hardware is a highly secure system. For protection against hackers it can generate a One Time Pin, which leaves less margin for error. If you want to keep tabs on your dealings, the wallet includes a transaction log. This feature records all the BTC entering or leaving the wallet.

You can visit Bitcoin.org to view a list of verified websites that offer to open wallets and transact for customers who enrol. The sites vary, and some of the latest features include multi-signatures which allow more than one person to get into a single wallet.

You get in with a password, called a security key, or a collection of keys. The most secure way is to store a key printed out on paper, then keep this hard copy in a safe place. That way, no hacker can get at it.

At first, I had imagined that I could find an ATM dedicated to Bitcoin and simply use a debit or credit card to buy some coins. These are very new in South Africa, but plentiful in the USA. But I soon discovered that you can easily buy Bitcoin at websites such as coinbase.com where clients from anywhere in the world can fund their account. Although some sites have paywalls, you can easily use the free trials to successfully buy and begin trading Bitcoin. Much like signing up for any online account, you will be required to fill out minimal information, and then you may fund your account via credit card or an electronic funds transfer.

So, I got my wallet and entered the world of Bitcoin. But as I made my first tentative trades, I encountered a new mystery. My grandfather had wanted to know where Bitcoins came from, and now I was wondering who controlled the flow of BTC around the world, in and out of nations and economies. When I asked someone who had been studying cryptocurrency for years, he told me that the entire system was controlled by blockchain.

Ah-ha! I thought. So Bitcoins are administered from this blockchain, which must be a big place, a huge building with a classical portico, perhaps, or a glass skyscraper. I reasoned that this blockchain was the Bitcoin equivalent of the Bank of England, the US Federal Reserve, or the South African Reserve Bank.

I asked my crypto expert friend, 'So where is this blockchain located – in Japan?'

And he was polite enough not to mock my innocent misconception. With a slight smirk, he explained that blockchain was 'everywhere', that it has no physical presence, and exists as decentralised software on millions of computers, world-wide. 'There's no building,' he said, 'and no staff.'

I had realised that blockchain was causing a disruption, a revolution that was going to change the way the world worked, and Bitcoin was only part of it.

'Imagine a book of account, a ledger written in computer language. And each page of this ledger is a block, with all the details of a business deal recorded on it. The next transaction adds a new connected block, and the chain of blocks gets longer and longer. Every new block contains a hash (a far shorter, seemingly random sequence of letters and numbers) of the previous network block. As a result, ever since the first block appeared on the network in 2009, called the Genesis Block, there has been a chain of transactions, all of which are included in various blocks. If you wish to check a particular transaction, you can search the blockchain right back to the Genesis Block. Because the blockchain can never be altered or deleted. It was designed to run automatically for all time, without human intervention.'

I began my study of the blockchain, and before long I had realised that it was causing a disruption, a revolution that was going to change the way the world worked, and Bitcoin was only part of it. It is becoming important to understand the potential of the blockchain. You need to take back freedom in your life, not just from a financial perspective, but also in the way you use services, platforms, technologies – and more importantly, how you look at the world.

Everywhere you look, you'll find fraud, corruption, mismanagement, financial restrictions, limited free speech and many other things that should not be issues in this day and age. When Satoshi Nakamoto created Bitcoin, the idea was not only to create a new disruptive technology, but also to show everyday people that there are solutions available to decentralise our entire lifestyle. And these solutions are based on the blockchain, which acts as a Bitcoin bank. Anyone with an internet connection is able to use it. The backbone of most financial systems is a ledger system where financial transactions are recorded, yet the system remains fraught with fraud, double transactions and identity theft.

Despite being distributed across a large network, it is impossible for a single person to corrupt the network; its millions of users ensure this.

This chapter is about the invention that made cryptocurrencies possible. Blockchains do not belong to a single institution, person or entity; in fact, the blockchain is essentially stored across a huge number of computers. The information is decentralised and distributed across the network. Despite being distributed across a large network, it is impossible for a single person to corrupt the network; its millions of users ensure this. Each record is a block – a user can view a block, and even add a new block. But it's impossible to change existing information. The blockchain has an additional layer of safekeeping in the form of cryptography, or secret code, which ensures records aren't counterfeited or altered.

Each transaction within a blockchain is known as a block.

Various people around the world validate Bitcoin transactions and earn a small fee in the process. The blockchain authenticates ownership of digital cash and makes it known that only one person claims it as his or her property. Within the blockchain, trust is manufactured through a ledger that is transparent and visible to all its users. The software is impossible to hack or change. If anyone tries to tamper with a block, it shows immediately because the system is decentralised, irreversible and easily available to its network and users.

The blockchain has minimum joining requirements. It is secure and costs less, which means that it has the potential to improve poor and struggling economies. The emergence and growth of the blockchain has been likened to the rise of the internet because it has the potential to transform how the financial system operates within the poorest of societies. The blockchain protects a user's identity while it guarantees an autonomous vehicle to conduct transactions in a world that grows more dependent on the internet. Despite being anonymous, the blockchain ensures a level of accountability and limits fraudulent activity. The world is moving toward a situation in which convenience is achieved through devices. The world transacts using apps, and a digital currency seems like a logical step. Ironically, we are using a Space Age version of the Stone Age peer-to-peer system.

CHAPTER ELEVEN: KEY LESSONS

1. Blockchain is a form of online ledger. It consists of records known as blocks, linked in a chain just like railway rolling stock. Each block refers to the one that came before it, in a so-called hash. This is an encrypted summary of the transaction in the previous block.

2. It is open to anyone. Blockchain analysts use this ledger to trace the history of whatever changed hands in each block. This need not be Bitcoin, for a blockchain can record almost anything: ownership of such property, or intellectual copyright, industrial contracts, even birth certificates.

3. It cannot be altered or erased. There is no such thing as creative bookkeeping with blockchain, because the facts are recorded for all eternity. Users may add a block, but cannot remove it. There is no possibility of changing your mind.

4. Millions of decentralised computers operate the blockchain. It resides 'in the cloud' and is everywhere and nowhere. It's impossible to hack or destroy because it exists on too many devices.

5. The blockchain is protected by encryption and many other fail-safe systems. Like the human body, it is a self-regulating system. Unlike the human body, it will never pick up a virus, get sick or shut down. Its design is far too robust for that.

TWELVE

Crypto security

A large part of the time I spent researching all the ins and outs of Bitcoin went into an investigation of security, and the possibility of things going wrong. And the worst thing would be your own fault: losing your private key. My blood runs cold when I contemplate that disaster, and that's why I have plenty of backups in various forms.

If you don't back up your private key and you lose it, you can no longer access your Bitcoin wallet to spend funds. As I learned when I was setting up my wallet, there is also a public key. This caused me some confusion, as I had assumed that a Bitcoin wallet address and the public key were the same. The woman who first briefed me on my wallet explained that the two keys are different, even though they are related mathematically.

I listened carefully as she told me, 'A Bitcoin wallet address is a hashed version of your public key. Every public key is 256 bits long and the final hash – which is your wallet address – is 160 bits long. The public key is used to ensure that you are the owner of an address that can receive funds.'

I asked her, 'Those numbers – could the bad guys hack their way into them?'

She smiled. 'Impossible! The public key is mathematically derived from your private key, but using reverse mathematics to work out the private key would take the world's most powerful supercomputer many trillion years.'

I quickly learned how easy it was to keep tabs on the figures in my wallet because it gives me an overview of my spending and receiving habits. My wallet stores a separate log of all my incoming and outgoing transactions. Last but not least, it also stores my user preferences, which depend on the wallet type and the platform. I started off with the Bitcoin Core client, which has so few preferences to tinker around with that I easily got the hang of it. All wallets generate a 'master' record where all of the preceding details are saved: the wallet.dat file. Make sure to create one or multiple backups of this wallet.dat file on other storage devices, such as a USB stick or memory card. The Bitcoin wallet software will let you import a wallet.dat file in case your previous file is damaged or lost, restoring your previous settings, including any funds associated with your Bitcoin wallet address.

If you don't back up your private key and you lose it, you can no longer access your Bitcoin wallet to spend funds.

When you take paper money out of a bank machine, you need to put it somewhere. This is usually in your wallet or your purse. Bitcoins also need to be stored somewhere, allowing you to access them when you want. As discussed briefly in the previous chapter, several variations of Bitcoin wallets are available, such as software wallets, hardware wallets, paper wallets, and web wallets. The private key to your Bitcoin wallet is the most important piece of information that has to be kept safe and secure at all times. This 'secret number' allows Bitcoins in your wallet to be spent, as it is used to verify that you are the legitimate 'owner' of the coin balance associated with your wallet address. A Bitcoin wallet, regardless of whether it is installed on a computer or mobile device, can contain more than one private key, all of which are saved in the wallet.

A software wallet is a Bitcoin application that sits on your computer's hard drive and allows you complete control and great security, because each Bitcoin you hold is only accessible on your own computer. This software, called Bitcoin Core, is developed and supported by the Bitcoin Foundation. When your software wallet is installed, it creates the wallet.dat file that holds the data that relates to your personal Bitcoin wallet. To find out how to get a software wallet, visit http://Bitcoin.org and click the Get started with Bitcoin link.

The Bitcoin software wallet is open source, meaning that the code is fully accessible by anyone who wishes to see it. Open source ensures transparency and allows users to check the source code to ensure it contains no malware or other suspicious code that could damage your computer or jeopardise your security. It also means, if you're a bit of a technical whiz kid, you can compile applications. A company called Prypto offers a product called the Crypto wallet, with two cards. One is your Bitcoin address, and the other is your private key, covered up by a scratch-off film (so, until it is removed, nobody knows what it is). This adds an extra security step to help keep your Bitcoins safe and sound.

This chapter on security is an important one, with the imperative: don't ever lose your Bitcoin key. If you do, that money will be forever stashed in cyberspace, where no one will ever get at it, including you. Some companies offer Bitcoin wallet services. They effectively act as a middleman to hold your Bitcoins and allow you to spend and deposit as you want, taking responsibility for the administration and security of your account. It also means that the company will ask you for personal information, thus making this an environment that is not anonymous. But, if you intend to use a third party Bitcoin wallet, ensure that you can trust the company behind the service. In the past, there have been several companies that held Bitcoins for people, but which have rapidly disappeared, been hacked, or gone bust. In general, exchanges or other third party companies that hold funds on your behalf should be treated with caution.

The country where the company is registered will have its own requirements as to how well regulated that company must be. The regulations of Bitcoin as a financial service or product are still being developed in many areas of the world. Which means that you should choose a country with a strong background in regulating financial services, such as the United States, United Kingdom, or the Isle of Man. While regulations are being developed, you should really exercise extreme care when storing funds on a third party exchange or similar company. Don't store any more than you need or more than you can afford to lose should the worst come to pass.

When you take paper money out of a bank machine, you need to put it somewhere. This is usually in your wallet or your purse. Bitcoins also need to be stored somewhere, allowing you to access them when you want.

CHAPTER TWELVE: KEY LESSONS

1. The Bitcoin key is so secure that it cannot be hacked in meaningful time, even by a consortium of supercomputers, working for centuries. You are the greatest security threat. To avoid losing your money for ever, back up your private Bitcoin key. There is absolutely no way a lost or forgotten key can be recovered. This provides the ultimate in security for your online wealth, so long as you have several backups, and behave responsibly.

2. If you must use a third party in your Bitcoin trading, choose a company in a jurisdiction with tough financial regulations. That will give you some protection.

3. Don't store your cryptocurrency in a site belonging to someone else for longer than a few hours. This is less secure than your own wallet and brings the old banking middleman back into the picture, to say nothing of the fees he charges.

4. The Bitcoin wallet is a great invention, and easy to use. It is secure and will keep your crypto wealth away from any type of hacker.

THIRTEEN

Trading ups and downs

The world of blockchain and Bitcoin was very exciting, and I could see many opportunities which included trading, one of the best ways of making money. The Bitcoin price is volatile, and dedicated investors can predict price increases or decreases. A successful Bitcoin trade can allow you to make a substantial amount of money; the opposite is also true. Be careful of how you trade and who you trade with.

There were times when I was trading that I felt I could have done a little more research. The wild volatility would leave me gasping in amazement. Sometimes the price of BTC screamed skyward, only to drop like a stone within hours. But the overall trend was upward. At certain moments I felt that I should have waited a little longer before diving in head first and expecting a winning lap. But that's what faith does to you – you trust something so much that you go all in with little or no doubt.

Currently there are a few merchants who accept Bitcoin, which can be directly converted to fiat currency such as ordinary paper notes or deposits. You need to be aware of the fact that the same factors which affect a fiat currency can also change Bitcoin prices. Should there be a major vote of no confidence against it, or should factors such as hacking and corruption affect it, the price will go down. That's why it is wise to approach everything with caution, including Bitcoin. Never commit more than you can afford to lose.

There were times when I was trading that I felt I could have done a little more research. The wild volatility would leave me gasping in amazement.

Using Bitcoin allows you to trade in several different ways. Because Bitcoin is well known for its volatile nature, there are gains and losses to be made each and every day. Sometimes those losses or gains will be big, and at other times they may be tiny. Even though quite a few merchants accept Bitcoin payments, nearly all of the funds are converted to fiat currency directly. This is done in order to protect the merchant from any Bitcoin price volatility that may occur. And it's one of the reasons why so many shopkeepers are happy to join the digital currency train. On the other hand, these conversions from Bitcoin to fiat currency also create a side effect as there will be selling pressure across the major exchanges. Bitcoin payment processors need to put those Bitcoin payments through as soon as possible to pay the right amount to the merchant.

I was happy playing the Bitcoin game, but I soon discovered that there were many other crypto coins that were trying to overtake Bitcoin. These alternatives are known as altcoins. They seek to improve on the ideas Bitcoin represents. Some people feel the need for more anonymity, while other developers want to explore the boundaries of the underlying blockchain technology. Rather than submit their ideas to Bitcoin developers, they prefer to use the free open source Bitcoin code, change the name, make some minor tweaks, and launch it as a brand new digital currency.

This chapter stresses the dangers of overly enthusiastic speculation, especially in the light of extreme volatility, and also with altcoins. Over the years, only a dozen or so altcoins have managed to stay relevant, mostly thanks to a strong community and the integration of some unique features that have not made it to the Bitcoin core (yet). Nevertheless, none of these altcoin communities is as large or as supportive as the Bitcoin world. But that doesn't mean there is no speculation going on in the altcoin scene. This is the reason why so many day traders prefer to speculate on the altcoin markets, as there is a lot of room for quick profits and quick losses. A few altcoins that have developers who are actively working include Litecoin, CasinoCoin and Guldencoin.

There are dangers in altcoin dealing. Rather than push up the price by buying coins, some unethical developers encourage community members to put down a lot of money for a valueless altcoin. And once the price is high enough, these developers cash out, take their money, and work on a new coin for the next week. There are many altcoins to go around, and most of them will never serve an actual purpose. However, if you can catch a few cheap coins before the price increases, there is a nice amount of profit to be made. But never become too greedy, as prices can plummet even faster than they rise. As the con artist said: 'Greedy people are the legitimate prey of guys like me, and who is guilty of the greater sin?'

CHAPTER THIRTEEN: KEY LESSONS

1. Not all altcoins are rip-off schemes. If you're determined to ride the market like a cowboy, don't risk more than you're prepared to lose. Do your research, keep in touch with cryptocurrency prices and trading trends. This also applies to the more popular cryptocurrencies, such as Bitcoin or Ethereum.

2. Remember, altcoins are a high-risk investment. High risk may mean big profits or equally big losses. Never double up into a losing streak, as the old gambler said. That's the quickest way to destroy a family fortune.

3. Bitcoin may be volatile, but it's safer than many altcoins because it has a record of continuous growth, despite violent ups and downs from time to time. It has proved itself already in a young market. Think carefully before you go for an unknown coin.

4. Some altcoins have been deliberately launched as part of a 'pump and dump' scheme, where the only guys to profit are the ones who started it up. Choose your exchange very carefully.

5. Beware of jurisdictions with lax financial regulations. These places attract scamsters who exploit regulatory loopholes to fleece innocent and unwary investors.

FOURTEEN

Blockchain secrets

P ut simply, the blockchain is a publicly distributed ledger offering unprecedented transparency regarding the Bitcoin ecosystem. It is a collection of all Bitcoin transactions since its inception in 2009. Every additional transaction is also logged on the Bitcoin blockchain. I understood all that as my research continued. But there were more astonishing revelations to come as I delved into the mysteries of the technology. Bitcoin is the least of what blockchain can do. The blockchain is a technological advance unlike anything seen before, and its decentralised nature means there is no central point of failure that can bring it down.

Because each new page in the public ledger contains a summary of the previous page or pages, it follows that the size of those pages will increase. That's exactly what happens to the size of the blockchain as more data is stored within it. Bitcoin's blockchain is most widely known as a record of all Bitcoin transactions of the past, present and future. Not only is the blockchain a bookkeeping tool, it also presents unprecedented transparency for the financial ecosystem.

And it is that level of transparency which many traditional financial institutions fear. They don't like to disclose numbers and statistics, whereas the Bitcoin blockchain is completely transparent in that regard. However, there is still a level of anonymity attached to the Bitcoin blockchain, as individual users or companies are represented by a Bitcoin wallet address, rather than by a name or address.

Not only is the blockchain a bookkeeping tool, it also presents unprecedented transparency for the financial ecosystem.

Consider the Bitcoin blockchain, from a financial point of view, as a shared database of transactions. Every Bitcoin node (a computer constantly running the Bitcoin wallet software to detect and validate new Bitcoin transactions) on the network owns a full copy of Bitcoin's entire transaction history, from the beginning (2009) right up to now. In the future, more and more transactions will be added on top of the existing blockchain, creating a timeline of exactly how Bitcoin evolved in the financial world.

Additionally, every new Bitcoin block is generated in chronological order, as it contains the hash of a previous block. Otherwise, this hash would be unknown, which would lead to the block being rejected by the network. Furthermore, Bitcoin network blocks of the past cannot be altered, because that would mean any block following a specific block number would have to be regenerated. That functionality is not available, nor will it ever be. As a result of keeping a public ledger containing all of the previous Bitcoin transactions between 2009 and the time you are reading this book, the blockchain continually grows in size. By the time you read this, Bitcoin will have surpassed a 50GB blockchain size by quite a margin. And as more and more transactions are broadcast on the Bitcoin network, the block size will have to increase, leading to an even larger blockchain file.

I began to study the new science of blockchain analysis. It is being developed by expert coders and is an entire new market within the Bitcoin ecosystem, which has been made possible because of the blockchain's transparent nature. Whether or not blockchain analysis will be a curse or a blessing remains to be seen, as the opinions are quite divided at this time. One thing that helps Bitcoin thrive and grow as a mainstream payment method is the acquisition of insights into how people are spending Bitcoins, not just in terms of which products and services are being bought, but also how long people are holding on to the coins that they receive in their wallet. Just like cash, Bitcoin is meant to be a payment method that can be spent anywhere at any time. Having a detailed analysis done on how long people hold on to their coins could help stimulate Bitcoin adoption all around the world. And that, in a nutshell, is what blockchain analysis does.

The positive side to blockchain analysis is not hard to find. Bitcoin is still a very young and immature financial system, and detailed analytics give industry experts valuable insights into how things can be taken to the next level, by answering questions such as: how are Bitcoins being spent? Where are the most new wallets coming from? Is the hoarding problem being addressed, or is it growing worse? All these questions deserve a proper answer, which is where blockchain analysis comes into the picture.

It is no secret that some of the 'oldest' Bitcoins recorded on the network have not been traded in years. Some people claim these coins belong to Satoshi Nakamoto, the creator of Bitcoin. Others argue that these were early adopters who simply forgot about Bitcoin after a while and never came back. Or maybe the private key was lost during a hard drive crash and never recovered, making the funds associated to those wallets 'unspendable'.

Making Bitcoin more user friendly is another hurdle that can be overcome by focusing more efforts on blockchain analysis. For example, some users would find it pretty annoying to receive a text whenever they sent or received a Bitcoin transaction. Some major wallet providers already offer this functionality. But receiving an SMS helps novice users to keep tabs on their spending habits and Bitcoin balance.

The blockchain can be used for just about anything you can imagine: tracking packages all around the world in real time, creating copyright claims, fighting online piracy, and bringing an end to counterfeit products. These are just a few of the ideas made possible by using blockchain technology. Granted, the blockchain has become well known for its financial capabilities in terms of recording transactions.

Having a detailed analysis done on how long people hold on to their coins could help stimulate Bitcoin adoption all around the world. And that, in a nutshell, is what blockchain analysis does.

But it is important to remember that blockchain technology is more than Bitcoin the currency. Beyond the financial aspect of blockchain technology, the blockchain itself allows us to achieve much more than just a transaction ledger. Several projects are currently being developed that will allow tools such as smart contracts, digital transfer of ownership and even copyright claims to exist on top of the blockchain. For example, here are just two of the new items I came across.

Factom: this is a layer built on top of the Bitcoin blockchain. It is focused on recordkeeping and data storage (for example, healthcare records).

Storj: this is a software package which rewards users with Storj tokens for storing part of the blockchain on their computers. I found out that these tokens can then be claimed by the users to store some of their own data on the blockchain. Because of its transparent nature, the possibilities of the blockchain's technological use are nearly endless, and developers are only just discovering the tip of the iceberg in terms of the blockchain's potential. And the number of possible uses increases every day. Blockchain applications which have nothing to do with cryptocurrencies are on offer to local corporates, with the promise that record keeping and admin systems will be revolutionised.

In blockchain application development, most of the focus is currently on financial services. That is only normal, as Bitcoin is mostly focusing on bringing financial services to people in unbanked and underbanked parts of the world. Plus, the blockchain is best known for being an open ledger. What we do know is that various projects are currently in development, and the non-financial ones aim to improve various aspects of everyday life. However, until these applications are put into proper coding, they are only ideas and nothing more at this point.

The idea behind blockchain applications is very similar to that of Bitcoin itself: restoring power to the individual user without having to rely on centralised services or companies. The blockchain's decentralised and transparent nature offers unprecedented technological advantages. But I soon heard about a big drawback: the blockchain's technological power comes with a steep learning curve for developers, analysts and users. Creating blockchain applications is not easy. Even for coders, it takes a while to get acquainted with the parameters and API call associated with Bitcoin's blockchain. That's a tool used by developers to call on a specific operation within a platform or application.

This chapter is intended to serve as an introduction to a phenomenon which is already bringing about a revolution in our daily lives, with an impact that will equal or exceed that of the internet. The main aim of blockchain application development is to improve our everyday lives by bringing transparency and accountability to existing infrastructure. Especially in terms of the financial world, where both of these features are desperately needed.

There is still much room left for other areas of technology to be improved by adopting the blockchain, and the years ahead will give us a better indication of what we can expect. Any type of blockchain application can be developed using a wide variety of programming languages, including JavaScript, Ruby, Perl, and PHP. And there are also the mobile operating systems to take into account, as blockchain applications are more than welcome on Android, iOS, Windows Phone, and Blackberry operating systems.

Developing a proper blockchain-based application is a time-consuming process, as there is a lot of code to write and potential outcomes to take into account. On top of that, it takes quite a bit of funding to write a new blockchain application from scratch, because developers need to be paid for their efforts. Blockchain development is not a poor man's game. But this is not something to worry about in the Bitcoin world, for venture capitalist investment is still on the rise, despite the volatile Bitcoin price.

I believe the blockchain is all about creating communities and giving individual users choices they currently do not have. It is often like-minded individuals who share an idea of how something can be done better, who are drawn to each other. An obvious example would be those who create alternative cryptocurrencies, also called altcoins. As a result, blockchain development is not tied to one programming language, and diversification is one of the greatest assets for blockchain developers. Whether this community spirit continues as blockchain applications become more commercial remains to be seen. There are certainly some comparisons to be drawn with the current state of blockchain development and the very early days of the internet.

CHAPTER FOURTEEN: KEY LESSONS

1. Blockchain is still in its early stages; many have never heard of it. But applications are set for exponential growth. Large international companies are already offering systems based on blockchain to South African corporates.

2. It will bring about a sea change in the way we work, as the internet did. Blockchain applications will take over the manufacturing world, as well as the legal system, payrolls, academia and education. The openness will mean less fraud and more trust. Costs associated with the current outdated systems will be trimmed by blockchain efficiency.

3. For the moment, blockchain development is concentrated on the priorities of crypto currencies and finance. But it will eventually spill over into many other fields.

4. Writing blockchain code is difficult and expensive. But the advantages outweigh the disadvantages, and development continues apace, all over the world.

5. People who are locked into old systems dread losing out to blockchain. A worried European banking figure wrongly stated that blockchain and cryptocurrencies were based on anonymity. He said, 'We cannot have anonymity!' This was in the long-lasting era of tax haven anonymity which was exposed in the shocking Panama Papers. There will be no tax dodgers under open, decentralised, impartial blockchain.

FIFTEEN

What's Bitcoin good for?

I cannot stress enough how Bitcoin is an app for the future. Though new and relatively unknown, it is a sound investment that will grow people's wealth over time. By the time that everyone wants it, its value will be so high that not many will profit from it. That is why it is wise to get in on the revolution now. With its limited supply cap of 21 million coins (expected to be reached in 2140) and the current low Bitcoin price, there are ample opportunities to make a quick profit from investing in Bitcoin.

Trying to play the Bitcoin price market is absolutely fine, but keep in mind, as I have already said, that financial losses often come quicker than profits. Other forms of using Bitcoin as an investment vehicle exist as well. Investing in Bitcoin can be a part of a long-term plan, rather than an attempt at quick profits and losses. Bitcoin is still in the very early stages of development, having been around for only nine years. There is still a long way to go in terms of educating people about Bitcoin, which creates an investment opportunity in its own right.

Earlier in this book, I mentioned how I will unpack the various ways in which one can use Bitcoin, and I will now take Prypto's list as a point of departure:

1. Use Bitcoin as an educational tool. The main purpose of Bitcoin, as I see it anyway, has always been to educate people on the potential of the blockchain and how to take back full control of their lives. Not just from a financial perspective, but also in the way people use services, platforms, technology, and more importantly, how they look at the world. Everywhere you look, you'll find fraud, corruption, mismanagement, financial restrictions, limited free speech and many other things that should not be issues in this day and age. When Satoshi Nakamoto created Bitcoin, the idea was not only to create a new breed of disruptive technology, but also to show everyday people that there are solutions available to decentralise our entire lifestyle and avoid such nastiness as fraud and corruption. Up until now, most of Bitcoin's focus has been on the price and the financial aspect of the technology.

2. Spend Bitcoin for everyday needs – Bitcoin is an electronic form of payment, which is one of the many reasons so many people are attracted to this virtual currency. Over the past few years, more and more places have started accepting Bitcoin payments as an alternative form of payment due to lower costs, instantaneous transactions, and no risk of fraud or chargebacks. As a result, Bitcoin is becoming a viable form of payment, both online and in-store, at various locations throughout the world. The Bitcoin ecosystem is mostly used for sending funds around the world, which also means that commerce is a major factor in keeping the ecosystem alive. With so many different merchants to choose from – some of which can even be used for everyday goods and services – Bitcoin is slowly becoming a mainstream form of payment. One interesting option to spend Bitcoin comes in the form of services and companies that deliver food to your doorstep. The possibilities are endless.

3. Indulge in luxury expenses with Bitcoin. Bitcoin can also be used for less frequent purchases, such as flights and hotel bookings. One interesting phenomenon these companies have noticed is

how Bitcoin customers are willing to spend slightly more on their flights and hotel bookings. It could be that Bitcoin users are more comfortable spending larger amounts on travel, or perhaps they were just offered unfavourable exchange rates at the time. The exact reason for this remains a mystery for now, but it just goes to show that Bitcoin acceptance is beneficial to both merchants and consumers, regardless of what product or service they offer.

4. Support charities with Bitcoin. One of the most important aspects of life is having the opportunity to do social good for other people who need it the most. Bitcoin donations can be sent to various charitable organisations, including the Red Cross and Greenpeace. In fact, some charities will even help you with deducting the donation from your yearly taxes, even though the payment was made in Bitcoin. The biggest advantages Bitcoin brings to the table, in terms of charity, is how you can send funds directly to the people in need, rather than having to rely on third-party organisations. Bitcoin offers a great alternative payment method compared to credit cards and bank transfers. No personal details are required and no verification documents. You just simply deposit funds and start paying. Bitcoin transfers are fast and non-refundable, making them a perfect payment method for online service providers such as casinos.

5. Invest in precious metals. Although this is technically the same as looking at Bitcoin as an investment vehicle, very few people know that Bitcoin can be used to purchase precious metals, such as gold and silver. On top of that, various online platforms let users trade Bitcoin against the value of precious metals as a form of day trading, and some have seen great success over the years. Always do due diligence and look up the companies and their reputations before investing any Bitcoin.

6. Give it away. Bitcoin is a perfect gift for friends, family, and loved ones. Bitcoin is usable for this through many merchants,

most of which do not even accept Bitcoin payments directly. But through the magical power of gift cards, Bitcoin can be spent or gifted as a payment method.

7. Pay bills. The option of paying bills with Bitcoin depends on where you live. That said, there are multiple platforms in development that will let you pay any bill with Bitcoin in exchange for a small commission. Phone bills, utility bills and rates and taxes will be paid in Bitcoin in the not-so-distant future. Cellphone top-ups through Bitcoin payments have been possible for quite some time now, though this functionality is not available worldwide just yet.

8. Use Bitcoin as a social experiment. Are you very passionate about Bitcoin but find its current lack of usability rather disheartening? Why not go out and try to convince merchants and consumers about the benefits of Bitcoin? After all, growing the ecosystem one step at a time takes time and effort, and since there is no centralised authority to take care of the job, every Bitcoin community member has some responsibility to push Bitcoin adoption. All these are just a fraction of the possibilities you can experience with Bitcoin, and coming up with your own creative ways to use the virtual currency is of great value to the community. Whenever you have a chance to use Bitcoin, make sure to share your story with the community.

9. For the avid gamer, who gets his thrills from a water-cooled computer rig which cost him big bucks, Bitcoin can be a way to pay for upgrades. New games are constantly coming along, and they make even greater demands on the CPU in a gaming set-up. And the dedicated gamer will want to keep up with the very latest in processors, to say nothing of memory – as much as possible. Gamers may check world prices, look for bargains and clinch the deal in Bitcoin.

One of the most important aspects of life is having the opportunity to do social good for other people who need it the most.

CHAPTER FIFTEEN: KEY LESSONS

1. Bitcoin has barely begun its career as a viable currency.
2. Bitcoin has the potential to become a worldwide medium of exchange.
3. There is no corner of the financial world that Bitcoin cannot improve.
4. Bitcoin has the flexibility to handle small change and huge transactions.
5. Bitcoin is volatile because of supply and demand in the market.

SIXTEEN

Deepen your crypto knowledge

Finding out more information about Bitcoin, the blockchain, and how the digital currency is evolving can also be done away from the pages of this book, believe it or not. Quite a few resources are at your disposal, all of which are aimed at bringing you up-to-date information on the Bitcoin ecosystem. Here are a few I visited in my exploration of the planet Crypto.

1. The Bitcoin Wiki. Having an unbiased and independent source of Bitcoin information is a valuable asset to the virtual currency community, because there are constant changes, updates and new services popping up. One of the most commonly used sources for information on the internet is Wikipedia, and Bitcoin has its own subsection explaining all of the terminology in finer detail. On the Bitcoin wiki, you can find all sorts of information, ranging from info about creator Satoshi Nakamoto – even though he remains quite a mystery – to mining, running a Bitcoin node, and much, much more. Definitely a source to keep an eye on, as there is always something to learn about Bitcoin you didn't know yet.

2. One of the most popular places for Bitcoin debates and service reviews is Bitcointalk.org. This forum, dedicated to Bitcoin and created many years ago, is one of several which provide breaking news, project development, services and goods and much more. If there is anything regarding Bitcoin you want to have a healthy discussion about, the BitcoinTalk forums are a must-visit. That being said, not everything posted on the BitcoinTalk forums is Bitcoin-related. A dedicated section for alternate virtual currencies, including Litecoin, Dogecoin and others, is available as well.

3. Avid users of Reddit may already have stumbled upon the Bitcoin subReddit at some point in their online browsing careers. The Bitcoin subReddit is home to many discussions that can touch upon a variety of subjects: taking Bitcoin to space and why payment processors are charging so few fees on transactions. Many more debates are opened and closed on a daily basis there. But there's a downside to the Bitcoin subReddit as well. At the time of writing, censorship is plaguing this platform at an alarming rate, and moderators often ban people and remove topics. However, all in all, the Bitcoin subReddit is still a good place from an information point of view, even if the overall community reaches toxic levels every now and then. Check it out here: http://reddit.com/r/Bitcoin.

4. Bitcoin.org (and Bitcoin.com) for the most part, has been the 'home page' of Bitcoin on the internet. A brief explanation of Bitcoin, along with a few demo videos and wallet software download links, is what this portal is all about. Providing information in a useful and convenient manner, without overwhelming novice users, this website is a great way to present Bitcoin to the outside world.

One of the most commonly searched terms – when it comes to finding out more information about Bitcoin on Google and Bing – is 'Bitcoin.com'. Until a few months ago (at the time of writing), Bitcoin.com was a domain redirecting to an entirely different website and only recently became a portal for all things Bitcoin. In addition, and unlike Bitcoin.org, Bitcoin.com has added a news section, which is updated daily with fresh content and opinion pieces. Check them out here: http:// Bitcoin.org and http:// Bitcoin.com.

5. Any type of trend or niche would not remain relevant without a few dedicated news sites covering everything about the subject matter. In the case of Bitcoin, quite a few news blogs are out there, most of which are run as hobby projects and therefore are only updated every now and then. Bitcoin is still fairly new, and there is a lot of room for competition in the news scene. That being said, there are also dedicated Bitcoin news outlets. Bitcoin Magazine, Inside Bitcoins, CoinDesk, Bitcoinist, Bitcoin.com, and CoinTelegraph are the most popular ones. Every news site tries to cover news in a completely different way, providing users with multiple angles on the same stories quite regularly. The beautiful thing about Bitcoin is that everyone who is an active writer has their own take on things, and connecting seemingly random events makes the entire ecosystem so interesting.

Even though mainstream media have a habit of putting Bitcoin in a negative spotlight, there's more coverage on the topic of virtual currencies than ever before. And it's growing. The underlying technology is of great value to financial institutions and innovative companies, whereas Bitcoin as a currency can help citizens legally bypass capital controls enforced by governments. Although most of the Bitcoin focus remains negative, mainstream media is keeping a close eye on the progression made by virtual currencies. More and more people are aware of Bitcoin, and mainstream media outlets will have to keep up with this trend if they want to remain relevant. Multiple Bitcoin documentaries have been created, following the history of this disruptive virtual currency so far. Nearly all of these documentaries can be found online and are free to watch. It seems the main reason for putting together a Bitcoin documentary is not to make money. The aim is rather to create a visual medium for everyday consumers to see and experience how Bitcoin can, and will, change the world, one step at a time.

Having an unbiased and independent source of Bitcoin information is a valuable asset to the virtual currency community, because there are constant changes, updates and new services popping up.

Bitcoin is about more than just the current exchange price, but a lot of people want to focus their attention on keeping up to date with the current Bitcoin value. There are various sites where you can see the current Bitcoin price, the average trading volume and charts distinguishing between buy and sell orders. BitcoinWisdom is one of the most often-used sites. It aggregates data from various exchanges around the world, broken down across major fiat currency trading pairs. All information is free to use and updated in real time. The amount of Bitcoin being traded across the world is simply amazing.

CHAPTER SIXTEEN: KEY LESSONS

1. Cryptocurrencies show huge early growth, but this is NOT inflation. It is caused by speculation, as traders jump in and out of Bitcoin positions, taking profits, then buying into the next dip in prices. This was how I operated as a trader. Inflation occurs when money supply is allowed to run wild, and this cannot happen under blockchain. The slow rate of Bitcoin mining and the eventual ceiling ensure that inflation is impossible with a trustworthy cryptocurrency.

2. Politicians, especially the financially illiterate specimens, cannot tell the difference between BTC and a Ponzi scheme. That's why many regard the future of finance with suspicion. But bankers tend to know a good thing when they see it, and are already using blockchain and crypto, especially the coin called Ripple.

3. Despite negative media reports, cryptocurrency growth trend is steadily upward. Supply and demand create trading opportunities for quick profits. The media tend to call it a bubble when Bitcoin price heads skyward and write stories about a crash when it falls. But this is a simplistic and misinformed view of a complex process.

4. Bitcoin was designed as an investment, a store of value. It is not necessarily a get-rich-quick scheme. Patient investors who bought BTC in its early days and held onto the coins are looking at rich rewards.

5. Bitcoin can be made absolutely secure, safe from hackers and fraudsters. So long as you carry out judicious research and take cool-headed decisions, the BTC holder is protected against fraud in an open, decentralised system, built around fail-safe security.

SEVENTEEN

Getting in with the crowd

I listened with great interest to a lecture on crowdfunding. Crowdfunding can be useful to the businessman and also to the small-time investor. A campaign to raise money from a whole crowd of individuals allows the businessman to decentralise the funding process. The crowd becomes his backer, to provide money up front. By accepting Bitcoin as a payment method for his campaign, he can decentralise things even further and reach a global audience.

There are advantages for the guys in the crowd when it comes to pay-out time, considering the fact that Bitcoin is not taxable in most countries. Many people view it as a safe haven for 'tax free' funding. But when they convert the raised funds to paper money, they may be taxed on the profit, depending on the amount. It is also important to note that not every project is launched for the right reasons. Some unscrupulous characters view crowdfunding as a way to get some funds quickly, without ever having to pay it back. A genuine project will never claim to do something with the money that the company doesn't intend to fulfil.

A campaign to raise money from a whole crowd of individuals allows the businessman to decentralise the funding process.

Luckily for Bitcoin enthusiasts, most crowdfunding projects so far have been legitimate, and have delivered on their promises. Depending on what type of project you invest in as a face in the crowd, it may take additional time to reach your profit, especially if blockchain technology development is needed. Even though most platforms implement security against misuse, there is always a minor chance of a project not delivering on the promises made. But that has nothing to do with Bitcoin – it can happen with any type of crowdfunding campaign.

Whenever you help crowdfund a Bitcoin project, always determine whether you are entitled to some form of reward. Crowdfunding is not the same as buying a share of a company or product at a cheaper rate. It simply means you're willing to spend money in order to make someone else's dream come true, which may or may not include a reward. However, you should not partake in a crowdfunding campaign just for the reward. That's not why this system was invented in the first place.

In my investigation of the pros and cons of crowdfunding, I came across two financial terms that were new to me. They are: ICO (Initial Coin Offering) and IPO (Initial Public Offering). An ICO happens when potential investors are given the chance to purchase a part of an altcoin's total supply before the mining process begins. Most investors do so in the hopes of seeing the price per coin increase in the near future. An IPO takes place when a Bitcoin or altcoin company or project hopes to raise additional funds for its operations. Investors receive a share in the company and earn interest, paid out in recurring dividends. Both terms carry a slightly negative connotation in the world of Bitcoin crowdfunding, because multiple false promises and scam projects have been associated with ICO and IPO promises. That said, both are being used for legitimate purposes as well.

For example, whenever you're planning to create a new use for blockchain technology which creates its own coin (also known as a token), you are effectively holding an ICO. The investor will receive an amount of tokens to use on the new platform once it has been launched. Backers are offered a tangible reward, even though it may not come in a physical form. Whether these digital tokens will gain value over time completely depends on the success of the project. But they also incentivise backers to spread the word about a crowdfunding campaign, which will go a long way in terms of developing a successful platform. Investors – both small and large – like nothing more than some sort of return on investment, preferably sooner rather than later. Using an ICO/IPO may speed up the process depending on the size and nature of the project.

You're putting additional stress on yourself by investing in a project that involves an ICO or IPO. You will need to keep track of the progress and make sure you're given the coins you've paid for. A crowdfunding campaign with an IPO/ICO generates excitement and expectations. Remember, you might see the value of the project, but you're also speculating, and you might become impatient to see some money. The individual crowdfunder often prefers buying a share in the company, with the prospect of getting dividends at regular intervals. Some crowdfunded projects have made the offer even sweeter by paying dividends in cryptocurrency. Even though these amounts will be very small in the early days, investors will start to see some form of return. And it will give everyone in the crowd a hint of how the company is faring.

CHAPTER SEVENTEEN: KEY LESSONS

1. Crowdfunding has advantages for the sponsor and small investor. When crowdfunding is carried out honestly, both the entrepreneur and his supporting crowd make a profit.

2. Beware! Scam artists have been known to use this financing method. They 'pump' a crowdfunding project up, then 'dump' it, leaving a crowd of investors with empty pockets.

3. Before you commit to any crowdfunding scheme, check the financier's business record. He or she should be open to small investors asking probing questions about past enterprises.

4. Always ask: What's in it for me, and when do I get it? The crowd is there to make money. And not to help out some guy who wants to get started in business with empty promises.

5. Don't get too excited over ICO and IPO announcements. This a time for calm, cool appraisal of the terms and prospects. And apply the investor's watchword: never commit more cash than you can afford to lose.

EIGHTEEN

Meet the cryptocurrency top twenty

Once I gave a talk on Bitcoin in a township hall and when I had finished, asked for questions. They came thick and fast. One curious young man asked me how many flavours of cryptocurrency were available. I tried to give him a short summary of the 'top twenty' coins. Some time later, I took the recording of my answers and used it to prepare this outline. And indeed, there's a world of 'flavour' waiting to be explored.

Bitcoin is the first cryptocurrency to be invented. It was dreamed up by a person (or maybe a group of IT experts) using the name Satoshi Nakamoto. This invention was intended as a replacement for the antiquated system we have inherited from the past. Cryptocurrency was designed to be more transparent and decentralised, without loopholes for fraudsters to exploit. One of Nakamoto's aims was to prevent a recurrence of the 2008 financial crash.

Bitcoin uses blockchain technology, which is an enormous network of computers, acting as a virtual supercomputer. Stored indelibly in this huge entity are blockchains. Each is literally a chain of software blocks containing data and information relating to coin balances and transactions. Special computers connected to the blockchain solve complex algorithms to verify all transactions that take place on the network.

Blockchain technology is what makes Bitcoin a better monetary system than our current one. It cuts out all the middle men, making payments cheaper and faster.

They also 'mine' fresh cryptocurrency. They do this by generating blocks of Bitcoin in return for the work they do. Unlike regular currency, where governments keep on printing money as they please, the Bitcoin money supply can only ever be 21 million coins. This makes Bitcoin inflation-proof, just like gold. And just like gold, it is very difficult to 'mine' a bitcoin because of the complexities of the algorithms. And that is where the term 'mining' comes from, because Bitcoin can be directly compared to gold – in the sense that it takes a lot of energy to make it available.

Blockchain technology is what makes Bitcoin a better monetary system than our current one. It cuts out all the middle men, making payments cheaper and faster. This technology also provides much better transparency, as transactions are made available to everyone and are verified by miners. It is also a global currency which opens up new possibilities, allowing anybody to transact and trade without needing any bank, permission from any government or anyone else. All they need is just themselves, a smart device and the internet.

ETHEREUM

Ethereum was invented by a young man named Vitalik Buterin. And now, as I write, Ethereum is the second biggest cryptocurrency in terms of both popularity and market value. Ether is the token used as the standard unit of measure of value in the Ethereum blockchain. This token provides the same solutions as Bitcoin and other cryptocurrencies. Vitalik was inspired by the blockchain technology behind Bitcoin. He then decided to create a new cryptocurrency. He wanted to take advantage of blockchain technology, create new possibilities and solve more problems, on top of those Bitcoin was already solving. The Ethereum platform allows you to create and customise tokens without needing to know how to code, as well as to write apps on the platform. Businesses can also use this platform to create smart contracts, cutting out lawyers. With such abilities, this platform can revolutionise the way people do business

RIPPLE

Ripple was created for the main goal of having cheaper, real-time international money transfers. Japanese banks are big fans of Ripple. Financial institutions don't want to use a payment system that takes too long to process transactions. They don't want to be hurt by any up-and-down exchange rates during the waiting period. Ripple certainly speeds things up, with real-time cross border payments. It lowers the risk of losing on an exchange rate that changes during the transfer process. With Ripple, there is no mining process involved, unlike Bitcoin. This makes it cheaper because there is no need for high computing power, which means less electricity is needed to process transactions.

BITCOIN CASH

This is the coin that was created to be better than Bitcoin. It was made to fulfil the original promises of Bitcoin. There were concerns that the underlying technology of Bitcoin could not be changed to make improvements. So Bitcoin became slower to process transactions as more users got into the Bitcoin market. What that meant was that more time would be needed for supercomputers to validate transactions. More electricity was now being consumed, making it more expensive to process transactions.

On 31 August 2017, a fork on the Bitcoin blockchain was created. The aim was to set up a new path on a blockchain that would enable programmers to update and improve the system. Past transactions would still be in record, as blocks are permanent on the blockchain. Essentially, what these programmers did when they made this fork, was to establish a new cryptocurrency, which was named Bitcoin Cash. Everyone who was in possession of Bitcoin on that day received the same amount of Bitcoin Cash on that date. The idea was to encourage Bitcoin users to use Bitcoin cash, because it is faster and cheaper.

Each block on the Bitcoin blockchain has a maximum size of 1MB per block. This limit slowed down the mining process because it took longer for the miners to verify transactions. The new fork, which resulted in Bitcoin Cash, can be updated with new rules, so the maximum block size on that fork was set at 8MB per block. This made it possible for miners to process data faster.

CARDANO

Cardano is led by the former CEO of Ethereum, Charles Hoskinson. Cardano provides a technological platform capable of using regular day-to-day financial applications, smart contracts and decentralised applications. With regard to financial applications,

Cardano's vision is to embrace a collection of design principles, engineering best practices and avenues for exploration. These principles and practices include (among other things) separate accounting and computation layers. Cardano has the ability to upgrade post-deployed systems without destroying the network. It provides a healthy middle ground for regulators to interact with commerce – but without compromising some core principles inherited from Bitcoin.

LITECOIN

Litecoin was created by Charlie Lee who is an ex-director of engineering at Coinbase and a former Google engineer. Litecoin was created to be better than Bitcoin in terms of speed and transaction costs. Charlie's goal was to create a coin that would be more suitable for smaller transactions and cheaper items. It uses blockchain, therefore provides the same solutions as Bitcoin and other cryptocurrencies. But it is four times faster than Bitcoin and has a maximum of 84 million coins that can be mined.

NEO

Neo uses blockchain technology, so it provides the same solutions as Bitcoin and other cryptocurrencies. What makes Neo unique is how it uses its blockchain for tangible assets. Neo's blockchain has the ability to digitise tangible assets by giving them unique digital identities. This allows users to transfer rights to properties, cars – anything you can think of – on the platform. Just as funds are verified by miners in the Bitcoin blockchain, transfers and ownership of assets can be verified in the same way. In fact, the process is much cheaper and more efficient than traditional methods. These digital identities also enable assets to be protected by law. The Neo platform has created even more possibilities and gives us one more reason to invest in future currency. In addition to giving digital identities to tangible assets, Neo is also a platform for smart contracts with increased privacy. Smart contracts on the Neo platform are kept in private storage.

NEM

The technology used behind this coin is also blockchain. In terms of transactions, this coin is a lot faster and cheaper than Bitcoin. However, the maximum number of coins that can exist have already been mined from the inception of this coin, which is 8 999 999 999 XEM. To gain access to these coins, they have to be harvested as accounts already have vested XEM. Harvesting is the act of forming blocks and harvesting can only be done by harvesters. The parties who own accounts with at least 10,000 vested XEM are the only ones who qualify as harvesters. Harvesters act as the 'miners' in the NEM platform, as they earn transaction fees for validating transactions on the blockchain and forming blocks.

SBI Sumishin Net Bank, Japan's largest trust bank, is a big fan of NEM. When it started getting involved with this coin, XEM gained some level of trust in the cryptocurrency market. However, there is a problem with the way it works. Theoretically, there can only be a maximum of 899 999 harvesters, but in reality, there are very few because harvesters do not own exactly 10 000 XEM. Their account balances will increase as they keep earning transaction fees. This makes this system undesirable as it can potentially become centralised. In addition, there is likely to be a future fork on this blockchain to resolve this issue.

IOTA

IOTA was founded by both David Sønstebø, who is a serial entrepreneur, and Dominik Schiener, the CEO at Fileyy. IOTA is a unique cryptocurrency that does not use blockchain technology. Instead, it uses a blockless distributed ledger called a tangle for its transparency. IOTA is designed in such a way that transfer can be done for free by eliminating the need to have miners to verify transactions. It is also the first coin with the ability to transfer value for free. The tangle technology makes it possible to establish a secure and authenticated communication channel between devices. This channel can then be used to transfer value. This innovation is what gives IOTA its value.

STELLAR

Keith Rabois and Matthew Charles 'Matt' Mullenweg are two of some of the big names that support Stellar. Keith Rabois is a technology entrepreneur and an executive member of PayPal and LinkedIn. Matt is a developer of WordPress. Stellar is different from most cryptocurrencies because it uses its own network of decentralised servers called the Stellar Network. It does have a global ledger, making all transactions just as transparent as that of a blockchain. How Stellar works is that it allows one to send regular currencies (USD, EUR, etc.) to peers, just as cheaply and efficiently as other cryptocurrencies. The receiving peer will receive funds in local currency. For example, if an American sends dollars to a receiver in Japan, Stellar will automatically select the lowest exchange rate available and convert the dollars into Japanese yen, which can then be withdrawn by the receiver. These Japanese yen credits are transferred in the form of Stellar tokens called lumens. These lumens cannot be further mined as the max have already been created and are being used to transfer actual money after being converted. Stellar does not have a profit motive because of the way it works. You cannot be a miner in the Stellar network because it is not blockchain and you cannot connect a supercomputer to validate your transactions. So you cannot earn transaction fees.

DASH

DASH was founded by Evan Duffield and its organisation is under the leadership of Ryan Taylor. Ryan Taylor is currently the CEO of DASH and is a former engagement manager at McKinsey. Like Bitcoin, DASH uses blockchain technology. In addition to the same solutions as that of the Bitcoin blockchain, DASH also gives one the option to make private transactions. This gives the user control over which transactions they want to keep a secret and which transactions they don't mind exposing. DASH also processes transactions faster and cheaper than Bitcoin.

MONERO

Monero uses blockchain, but the main difference between Monero and Bitcoin is that Monero is designed to be completely private. Transactions cannot be easily linked to any user. What the system does is break a transaction into smaller multiple transactions and then mixes them to make them untraceable. This platform is suitable for users who require complete anonymity when making payments, which would probably be high profile government officials or black market criminals.

BITCOIN GOLD

Similarly to Bitcoin Cash, Bitcoin Gold was created as a result of a hard fork on the Bitcoin blockchain. This hard fork was created for experimental purposes to use a new proof-of-work algorithm. The goal for Bitcoin Gold was to bring back the mining process through graphic processing units instead of ASIC. Bitcoin miners eventually started using ASIC to mine because they figured it was fast and consumed less power. However, what was really happening is that Bitcoin mining was becoming centralised. The mining process of Bitcoin is becoming more specialised and most people do not have access to supercomputers. Some countries do not even allow these supercomputers to operate because of the way they consume electricity. Distribution of mining equipment has become dominated by a very small number of entities, some of whom have engaged in abusive practices against individual miners and the Bitcoin network as a whole.

Bitcoin Gold is meant to provide an opportunity for countless new people around the world to participate in the mining process with widely-available consumer hardware that is manufactured and distributed by reputable mainstream corporations. This makes Bitcoin Gold more aligned to Satoshi Nakamoto's vision of a decentralised monetary system. The purpose for doing this is to make Bitcoin mining decentralised again. Satoshi Nakamoto's idealistic vision of 'one CPU – one vote' has been superseded by a reality where the manufacturing and distribution of mining equipment has become dominated by a very small number of firms.

ETHEREUM CLASSIC

This currency is the original Ethereum. In the beginning, Ethereum was using one chain which was called the DAO fork. This DAO fork was bugged and the price of Ether crashed, losing half its value. To resolve this matter, Ethereum was forked into two versions. The new token created during the fork adopted the name Ethereum, while the original tokens were still in demand and being used. This older version of Ethereum was then renamed Ethereum Classic. Ethereum Classic uses blockchain, just like Ethereum and Bitcoin. Just like Ethereum, Ethereum Classic blockchain is a platform that can be used to run smart contracts. Applications written using Ethereum Classic platform applications run exactly as programmed without any possibility of down time, censorship, fraud or third party interference.

QTUM

The most significant people involved in the development of Qtum are Anthony Diiorio and Roger Ver. Anthony Diiorio was a founder at Ethereum, as well as CEO & founder at Jaxx & Decental. Roger Ver is a Bitcoin start investor and is well known for promoting Bitcoin in various countries while Bitcoin was still new. Just like Ethereum, the Qtum blockchain can be used to build decentralised applications. In the case of Qtum, the decentralised apps created can also be executable on mobile phones and are still compatible with major blockchain ecosystems. With Qtum, it's easy to create your own token and smart contracts.

LISK

Lisk's mission is to also use blockchain technology for other functions, such as providing developers with the tools to develop decentralised apps using blockchain technology. This is quite similar to what Ethereum is doing, but the Lisk developer tools are more accessible. They have an SDK written in JavaScript, which allows Java developers to create decentralised apps on the blockchain.

RAIBLOCKS

This coin was developed by Colin LeMahieu, who was a software engineer at Qualcomm and National Instruments, and Zack Shapiro, who is an iOS developer and co-founder and former CEO of Luna. The technology behind Raiblocks is unique because it is designed in such way that it can provide the same solutions as other cryptocurrencies – for zero transaction fees. This is made possible by the way it is structured.

Raiblocks uses what they call a block-lattice structure, which is a structure made up of one blockchain for each user. Instead of having a system of one blockchain where all transaction information is shared to everyone connected to it, every user's transaction history is recorded on their own blockchain permanently. This blockchain is called an account-chain.

Since the account-chain can only be updated by its user, as he or she transacts, no miners are needed. The reason why miners are needed in Bitcoin is because they have to validate all transactions that happen on a huge blockchain shared by every user. With Raiblocks, miners are not needed since there is no shared blockchain. Secondly, transactions are instant. With Bitcoin, transactions reflect after roughly 10 minutes, as miners validate that transaction. That's why transaction fees are basically non-existent with Raiblocks.

SIACOIN

Siacoin uses blockchain technology, like most other crypto-currencies. But the technology behind Siacoin also provides cloud storage that is 10 times cheaper than current storage providers such as Amazon. Secondly, what Sia does in its cloud storage is that it splits apart the content users want to store. After splitting that content, it encrypts all those parts and then distributes them all over its decentralised network.

ZCASH

Zcash uses blockchain, but the platform behind this coin shields all transactions of the coins to hide the sender, recipient and the value of the transaction. This is what gives Zcash its value, because this kind of privacy is in demand in the cryptocurrency market.

STRATIS

This cryptocurrency depends on the usual blockchain technology. But it uses blockchain as a service. Companies use the Stratis platform to set up their own private blockchains. Therefore, they can transfer funds, use it for smart contracts, and do whatever they want to cater for their business needs.

CHAPTER EIGHTEEN: KEY LESSONS

1. There are many different forms and flavours of cryptocurrency. They were devised as imitations or improvements on the original Bitcoin dreamed up by Satoshi Nakamoto.

2. Some are more successful than others. Still leading the pack is Bitcoin and its derivatives, Bitcoin Gold and Bitcoin Cash.

3. Research deeply before you invest. Follow the market prices, stay alert and don't believe everything you hear. Buy on facts, not rumour.

4. Pick a reputable crypto that matches your needs. There are coins and systems which have strong points. For example, you could use Stratis to set up an in-house blockchain of your own. Perhaps use Neo to run a property firm or used car business.

5. Don't take a get-rich-quick attitude – invest! Crypto is going to be around indefinitely, and you can be rich in the fullness of time – if you're prepared to be patient and go for low-risk coin investments.

CONCLUSION

Stepping into the future

As I conclude my book, I would like to draw from my biggest goal in life and that is to ensure that people live out the best versions of themselves. Do not be afraid to stand out at all times. Dare to be different. We live in a world of risk, so we must learn to do some research before we take that leap into the unknown.

This book details the many leaps I have taken and the numerous times I have crashed to the ground. Painful as these experiments-gone-wrong may have been, each one was a learning experience, and I was able to move on. It seems the hardest lessons are the ones you never forget.

We are all standing on the threshold of a new world, and much of it will come as a complete shock, full of things we never imagined. But there will also be treasures and pleasures we didn't expect. I have a pretty good idea of how I got where I am today – but where I'll be tomorrow remains a mystery. And an adventure.

If anything, I hope that you will be able to see a vague shape of tomorrow's world through my adventures with cryptocurrency. So be curious, be inquisitive, be careful – and boldly step into the future.

A list of useful websites

The following is a list of useful websites that I compiled while I was learning as much as I could about Bitcoin and other currencies.

http://reddit.com/r/Bitcoin
www.bitcointalk.org
www.bitcoinwisdom.com
www.blockchain.info
www.coinbase.com
www.coinmarketcap.com
www.cryptotrader.com
www.localbitcoins.com
www.prypto.com

About the author

Mpho Dagada is a cryptocurrency expert, who specialises in Bitcoin. He has vast experience in the field. He is also the owner of Invest in Future Currency, which hosts online classes and live seminars to teach and educate the public about cryptocurrency. He is well respected as a hub of knowledge when it comes to cryptocurrencies.

He currently owns the company, NDA Logistics. Mpho established this professional transportation service company to offer excellent transportation and ensure a quality experience for clients. The company's footprint covers various regions across South Africa. He also owns and founded Foodz Holdings. This company focuses on building food brands that meet international standards. It is at the forefront in shaping the global future of the food industry in South Africa and across the global platform.

A natural leader, Dagada has taken part in public speaking from an early age. He has been awarded many accolades including best Public Speaker and Debater in Limpopo. Mpho does not leave anything to chance. He has also taken on a mentorship role by coaching and leading the Louis Trichardt debating team to a national level, where they excelled in their performance. Mpho was one of the national finalists of Young Communicators, which saw him winning funds towards a school project of his choice.

Among Mpho's numerous accolades, he boasts a colourful background in presenting, leading debates, chairing committees and outreach programmes. As a result, he was invited to an exchange program in Toronto, Canada, where he spent six weeks learning about other spheres of life and interacting with the global community. He was also nominated to represent South Africa at the One Young World International Summit in Zurich, Switzerland. During his time on radio, one of the things that he is proud of is designing an Anti-Xenophobia campaign for IOM (International Organisation of Migration). Mpho has been honoured with the President's Award, Bronze level.

Mpho was selected as one of the young entrepreneurs globally to participate in the prestigious TrepCamp which took place at Stanford University, in the US. In this program he went to visit and learn from Google, Facebook, Salesforce and many other companies in Silicon Valley. He presented his idea together with his group to Silicon Valley investors and accepted an award for making it into the top five.

Mpho is often invited as a public speaker to motivate and educate the public about entrepreneurship and lifestyle issues. He also speaks about his experiences in business and the key principles that have helped him become the innovative businessman he is today.